BRITISH UNTOUCHABLES

Monitoring Change in Education

Series Editor:
J. Mark Halstead
University of Huddersfield, UK

Change is a key characteristic of the worlds of business, education and industry and the rapidity of change underlines an urgent need to analyze, evaluate and, where appropriate, correct its direction. The series is aimed at contributing to this analysis. Its unique contribution consists of making sense of changes in education and in offering a timely and considered response to new challenges; the series, therefore, focuses on contemporary issues and does so with academic rigour.

Other titles in the series

British Untouchables
A Study of Dalit Identity and Education

PAUL GHUMAN
Aberystwyth University, UK

ASHGATE

Published by
Ashgate Publishing Limited
Wey Court East
Union Road
Farnham
Surrey, GU9 7PT
England

Ashgate Publishing Company
Suite 420
101 Cherry Street
Burlington
VT 05401-4405
USA

www.ashgate.com

British Library Cataloguing in Publication Data
Ghuman, Paul A. Singh (Paul Avtar Singh), 1936-
  British untouchables : a study of Dalit identity and
  education. -- (Monitoring change in education)
  1. Dalits--Great Britain--Social conditions. 2. Dalits--
  Education--Great Britain. 3. Children of immigrants--
  Education--Great Britain. 4. Caste--Religious aspects--
  Hinduism. 5. Dalits--Great Britain--Ethnic identity.
  I. Title II. Series
  371.8'29914041-dc22

Library of Congress Cataloging-in-Publication Data
Ghuman, Paul A. Singh (Paul Avtar Singh), 1936-
  British untouchables : a study of Dalit identity and education / by Paul Ghuman.
    p. cm. -- (Monitoring change in education)
  Includes bibliographical references and index.
  ISBN 978-0-7546-4877-2 (hardback) -- ISBN 978-0-7546-8968-3 (ebook)
  1. Dalits--Great Britain--Social conditions. 2. Dalits--Education--Great Britain. 3. Asians-
  -Great Britain--Social conditions. 4. Asians--Education--Great Britain. 5. Social classes--
  Great Britain. 6. Education--Social aspects--Great Britain I. Title.

  DA125.S57G527 2011
  305.5'6880941--dc22
                                                                        2010048849
ISBN 9780754648772 (hbk)
ISBN 9780754689683 (ebk)

Printed and bound in Great Britain by the
MPG Books Group, UK

Contents

Glossary of Terms

Achute	Untouchable, an Untouchable
Ad, adi	ancient, original
Ad Dharamis	those who follow the original religion of native Indians prior to the Aryan invasion; later on it became associated with the teaching of Guru Ravidas ji
Adi Granth	holy scripture of the Sikhs; also called *Guru Granth Sahib*
Adivasi	original dwellers; a name given to tribal people
Arora	a merchant class
Arti	ritual in which lighted lamps are waved in circles in front of Hindu deities
Arya	an ancient Indo-European people
Arya Samaj	Hindu reform movement of twentieth century
Avatar	manifestation of a deity or released soul in bodily form on earth; an incarnate Divine teacher (*OED*); incarnation of Vishnu and /or Krishna
Baba (ji)	grandfather or respectful title used for seniors
Balmiki (Valmiki)	followers of Rishi Valmiki, also called Churas of the (considered offensive) traditional occupation, sweepers
Batt	to speak English
Bhagat	literary devotee; Hindu and Muslim saints whose hymns are included in *Guru Granth Sahib*
Bhagavadgita (Gita)	a poem composed between the second century BC and the second century AD and incorporated into the *Mahabharata*; it stresses the importance of doing one's duty and faith in God (*OED*)
Bhakti	devotional worship directed to one supreme deity (*OED*)
Bhangra	a type of popular music combining Punjabi folk traditions with Western pop music (*OED*)
Bhatra Sikhs	a Sikh caste group in the Punjab; considered to be low-caste by the dominant Jat cast. They claim their descent from Brahmin lineage (see Thomas and Ghuman, 1976).
Bhavan	temple of Chamar caste; also building
Biraderi	extended family network; also refers to caste group
Brahmin/Brahman	a member of the highest Hindu caste, that of the priesthood (*OED*); also called twice born
Chamar	an Untouchable caste who were traditionally leather workers; the acceptable term for all Untouchables now

	is Dalit. Chamar in India is considered offensive. If this caste group hails from Gujarat they are called Moochis
Chamarli	separate area in north Indian villages where Chamars live
Chura	an Untouchable caste traditionally engaged in most menial work (sweeping, lavatory cleaning), which they consider very offensive
Dalit	oppressed people of India formerly called Untouchables; for wider use it is attributed to Dr Ambedkar
Dera	literally, a camp; a sacred compound
Dharm (Dharma)	in Hinduism, *dharma* is seen as the cosmic law both upheld by the gods and expressed in right behaviour by humans (*OED*); sometimes refers to religion or moral duty
Diwali	a Hindu festival of lights (*OED*), also celebrated by Sikhs
Gadar (Ghadar)	mutiny; a militant movement of expatriate Punjabis in North America in the twentieth century
Goras	white people
Gurdwara	a Sikh place of worship (*OED*); literally means guru's abode
Gurumukhi	literally from the mouth of the guru; the script in which Punjabi language is written in India
Guru Gobind Singh	the tenth guru b. 1666–1708
Guru Nanak	first Sikh guru b. 1469–1539
Guru Ravidas	saint of Bhakti movement belonging to Chamar caste; guru/saint revered by Chamars whose hymns are included in *Guru Granth Sahib* – the holy book of the Sikhs
Harijan	people of God; term coined by Gandhi for Untouchables
Holi	a Hindu festival celebrated in February or March in honour of Krishna (*OED*)
Ik onkar	God is one; opening of Japji sahib – the morning prayer of Sikhs
Izzat (izat)	family honour
Jai Bhim	greetings of the followers of Baba Sahib Bhim Rao Ambedkar
Jat	the dominant farming caste of rural Punjab and parts of North India
Jati	sub-caste; the practical manifestation of caste
Jawan	a soldier in Indian army
Jhir	a water carrier *jati*
Ji	used with names and titles to show respect (*OED*); for example, aunty ji and so on
Julaha	a weaver; the weaver *jati*
Karma	the sum of a person's actions in this and previous states of existence (*OED*); Punjabis often use it to refer to one's fate determined by deeds in the past life

Khalsa	the body or company of fully initiated Sikhs, to which devout orthodox Sikhs are ritually admitted at puberty; founded in 1699 by the last Guru Gobind Singh (*OED*); also literally pure
Khatri	an urban merchant caste in the Punjab and Haryana
Kshatriya	one of the two 'twice born' castes of Hinduism; traditionally a warrior caste
Langar	communal kitchen in a *gurdwara* where the communal meal is served; an innovation by Sikh gurus to overcome caste prejudice relating to purity rituals of Brahmins
Mahabharata	one of the two great Sanskrit epics of the Hindus, existing in its present form since about AD 400 (*OED*)
Mahar	a large Untouchable caste in Maharashtra; Dr Ambedkar belonged this caste
Mandir	Hindu temple
Manu	the legendary author of the traditional Hindu social code
Masjid	mosque
Mazhabi	literally religious; term used for Chura Untouchables who converted to Sikhism
Mochi	Gujarati *jati* who works with leather; in North India referred to as Chamar
Moksha	released from the cycle of rebirth impelled by the law of karma (*OED*)
Mukti	deliverance/salvation
Nirvana	a state of perfect happiness (*OED*)
OBC	also Other Backward Castes; in administration parlance, backward castes are defined as those whose ritual rank and occupational status are above Untouchables but who themselves remain socially and economically depressed
Panchayat	a village council; also caste panchayats are to be found in North India
Panth	a Sikh society
Prasad	blessed food
Pucka	Genuine; permanent; solidly built (*OED*)
Pursa/pursha	person
Quom	religious community; an ethnic group; a national group
Rajput	literally means sons of *rajas*; the dominant caste of the Punjab hills
Rama	the hero of the *Ramayana* and husband of Sita, widely venerated by some sects as the supreme god (*OED*)
Ramayana	one of the two great Sanskrit epics of the Hindus, composed in about 300 BC (*OED*)
Ramdasia	a name used for Chamars who convert to Sikhism

Ramgarhia Sikhs	Sikh artisan caste comprised of carpenters, blacksmiths and builders
Sabha	an assembly or society; a social or religious movement
Sadhu	a holy and good man
Salwar/Shalwar	a pair of light, loose, pleated trousers tapering to a tight fit around the ankles (*OED*)
Samaj	society, organization
Samosa	a triangular savoury pastry fried in ghee or oil, containing spiced vegetables or meat
Sangat	congregation in *gurdwara*; group, society
Sat Siri Akal	greetings of Sikhs; 'True is the Timeless Lord'
Satyagraha	literally, truth-force; a term coined by Gandhi to describe his agitation to gain independence; also conflict resolution
Sarpanch	the head of a village (*OED*)
Scheduled Castes	a neutral term promulgated by the British in 1936 to describe the Untouchables; this was retained and used by the architects of the Indian Constitution in 1950. Now it is widely used by judiciary and government bodies
Scheduled Tribes	a list of indigenous tribal populations who are entitled to the same treatment as scheduled castes
Shahid	martyr
Shiva (Siva)	god associated with powers of reproduction and dissolution (*OED*)
Shuddi	purification; an Arya Samaj rite affirming a person's Hindu purity
Singh	literally, lion; second name given to all male Sikhs so that they cannot be identified by caste
Sita	in the *Ramayana*, the wife of Rama, the Hindu model of the ideal woman, an incarnation of Lakshmi (*OED*; Lakshmi is goddess of wealth and knowledge)
Sr	term of respect
Swami	a holy man; a title implying spiritual achievement
Untouchables	those who are outside the Hindu *chaturvarna* (four castes system) now they are described as Dalits
Valmiki	author of the *Ramayana* (a Hindu epic) and considered to be a great kavi (poet). He is revered by his followers who were called by derogatory names such as *bhangis* and *churas*
Varna	the four Hindu castes: Brahmin, Kshatriya, Vaisya and Sudra (*OED*); literally colour
Vedas	The earliest Hindu texts
Vidya	knowledge
Zat	Urdu word used in the Punjab (including Pakistani Punjab) having the same meaning as *jati*

Acknowledgements

I wish to thank the following bodies for their financial support without which help the project would not have seen the light of the day. Firstly, Aberystwyth University which financially supported my small project which lead to planning of this large-scale study. Professor Noel Lloyd, the Vice Chancellor, further supported my endeavours by providing me with an office and ancillary facilities to complete the project.

Secondly, I thank the British Academy for supporting the project by generously funding my travelling and lodging expenses in the English Midlands. The Academy was supportive and understanding when due to an accidental leg injury I had to defer data collection for a year.

Lastly, I am indebted to the Dalit organizations that willingly provided me useful information and encouragement. They were kind and generous in their hospitality and allowed me to attend their committee meetings and invited me to their annual conferences which proved to be of immense value.

I wish to record my debt of gratitude to all the young people, parents, teachers, head teachers, school governors, community leaders, and temple and *gurdwara* priests who willingly participated in interviews and formal and informal discussions.

At a personal level I am grateful to Mohinder Paul Upal for his unstinting help in a variety of ways. Despite his busy schedules he was always willing to drive me to places of worship, interviewees' homes, and schools. His deep knowledge of Indian communities in the Midlands helped me to clarify my thinking on many controversial issues.

I appreciate the help and support of Susan and Robin Chapman for reading the manuscript and making helpful suggestions and comments to improve both the style and substance of the book. I thank Theresa Jarvis, my wife, for furnishing a comfortable study at home to work in, and showing genuine interest in the project.

I have sought advice and invited comments from many colleagues for which I am grateful. Despite the input and suggestions of colleagues and friends I am sure there are shortcomings as the book deals with many sensitive personal and social issues. I take full responsibility for the content of the book. I also wish to put on record that this project has broadened my understanding of the social and personal dimensions of one of the most pressing issues facing Indians both in the UK and in India.

List of Tables

List of Abbreviations

ACDA	Anti Caste Discrimination Alliance
BSP	Bahujan Samaj Party
BJP	Bharatiya Janata Party
NIESR	National Institute of Economic and Social Research
OBC	Other Backward Castes
SC	Scheduled Castes
ST	Scheduled Tribes
SGPC	Shiromani Gurdwara Parbandhak Committee
UP	Uttar Pradesh

A Note on Terminology

Nothing can be more distressing to oppressed and weak communities than being referred to by derogatory 'names' and 'labels' ascribed to them by dominant and powerful ruling classes. Traditional caste names can be very offensive and insulting to 'outcaste' (former Untouchables) people who as a group have been suppressed for over two millennia by high caste people.[1] For administrative purposes they were described as Scheduled Castes and Scheduled Tribes by the British in 1935[2] (see Dushkin, 1972). These terms have been retained and used by successive Indian Governments, since Independence in 1947. I have used the term Dalits (a Marathi word meaning oppressed ones) as it is now widely used in India. I have also used, almost interchangeably, the term 'Untouchables', as it is still widely understood outside India and resonates with many people and scholars who champion their cause for humanitarian treatment and justice[3] (Deliege, 1999; Mendelsohn and Vicziany, 1998; Jadhav, 2002). It is a sound conceptual category which refers to communities who are still suffering from multiple social and material disadvantages.

Dalits in the UK are composed of a number of communities. The majority of them are of the *Chamar* caste (former leather workers), many of whom call themselves *Ravidasis* – the follower of Guru Ravidas. A significant minority converted to a new sect/religion and called themselves *Ad Dharmis* (native religious people prior to the Aryan invasion). The other significant community in the UK prefers to call themselves *Valmikis/Balmikis*, the followers of Rishi Valmiki ji. Their traditional employment (scavenging) was considered to be the lowest among even the outcastes and they were called *Bhangi*, which is now considered to be most offensive – somewhat equivalent to the word 'nigger' used by whites for African Americans in the US and by some British army officers to refer to Indian sepoys during the British Raj. I have used the above 'terms' judiciously depending on the context and very much hope that they will not give offence. Furthermore, many interviewees in my study have used 'words and names' to describe their personal and/or social experiences which might be considered

---

1   Many scholars refers to them as caste Hindus (Srinivas, 2002; Michael, 1999).

2   According to Mendelsohn and Vicziany (1998: 4): 'The so-called Schedule is a list of castes entitled to parliamentary seats, public employment and special educational benefits. The Schedule Castes was originally promulgated by the British Government of India in 1936 but the term only became widely used after Independence.'

3   In India it is a criminal offence to use the world *Achute* or any other derogatory name to describe communities which were considered to be outside the Hindu caste system.

insulting and objectionable by some readers. However, to preserve the integrity of their comments I have retained such terms/labels and sincerely hope they will be understood in the context in which they are used.

Chapter 1

Introduction

This book presents a story of Indian Dalit communities who have settled in the English Midlands. I have written extensively on the problems of Indian and South Asian young people in the UK and North America. I thought that Dalit (formerly called Untouchables) young people should not be any different in their life styles, world outlook, and social adjustment than their peers of other castes. However, on one of my research trips to Birmingham, I happened to talk to a parent who identified himself as a Dalit. When I remarked: 'You mean *Harijan*', he insisted that he likes to call himself a Dalit (oppressed person) and explained that: 'Harijan is a condescending term coined by Gandhi who condoned "casteism", and we totally reject it.' We entered into further discussion and he told me that there is a serious caste problem in multicultural schools where a majority of the students are of Indian, Pakistani and Bangladeshi origins. He went on to narrate his own bitter experiences of caste prejudice and discrimination in India. He was not allowed to drink water from the water pump belonging to a high caste person and was made to sit outside the classroom by his teachers. Furthermore, high caste people in his village used him as an errand boy. In the UK he was discriminated against by Jat people in a *gurdwara* who told him he was told not to distribute *prasad* to the congregation, as he is not of pure caste.

Our exchanges brought back many memories from my childhood memories (1950s), which I have probably blotted out since I have lived in Britain for over 50 years. I recalled that we were told that Chamar (who originally worked with leather) farm workers were to use their own utensils for drinking and eating. Should they forget to bring these along, they were to drink water/lassi by cupping their hands. We had to avoid touching their cupped hands in case our jugs might become polluted and have to be purified by burning them with hot charcoal. I also remembered that even respectable Chamars were made to sit in lower positions (on stools) than high caste Jats and Rajputs. In our village there were many other indignities heaped upon them and their households, regarding which I now feel ashamed and partly guilty. Their status was put down to their karmas in previous lives. However, there were other farming families (including my mother's) who insisted that farm labourers should be accorded proper respect and dignity. They instructed their offspring to show them due respect by calling them baba, if elderly, and uncle, if they were older, and so on. Some even treated them as family members.

My case study of a village in the Punjab reveals that such slights and insults thankfully belong to a bygone era and that the material and social conditions of Chamars and Valmikis in villages have changed significantly, though it has been an uphill struggle. However, I was dismayed to read a summary of a research report in *The Hindu* (29 January 2010: 13) released by the Chairman of the Indian University Grant Commission. It is based on a survey of 1589 villages in Gujarat, India. According to its authors, the shameful practices noted above are still common in rural areas of Gujarat. I quote: 'The Dalit passengers were required to vacate seats in government owned State transport buses for non-Dalit passengers ... Even in tea kiosks, cups were separated for the Dalits and such customers were required to clean their own utensils ... Dalit students were not served water in schools. They were expected to go home or carry their own water with them.' It is clear that progress in abolishing caste discrimination in India is very patchy and it varies from region to region, for instance urban areas in north India are a great deal more progressive than rural areas in the south (see Chapter 2). Jadhav, a distinguished Dalit economist (2002: 3), makes a poignant comment in his autobiography:

> The 3,500-year-old caste system in India is still alive and violently kicking. In cities they will tell you, 'the Caste system is a thing of the past, it now exists only in villages.' Go to the villages, and they will tell you, 'oh no. Not here, maybe in some other village.' Yet open the matrimonial section of any newspaper and you will find an unabashed and bewildering display of the persistent belief in caste and sub-caste ... Consciously or subconsciously, Indians, whether in their own country or abroad, still make judgments based on caste.

The above encouraged me to read extensively on the subject. I was deeply moved and humbled by the personal sacrifices and struggles of Dalit leaders – especially of Baba Phule, Dr Ambedkar, Mangoo Ram, and Kanshi Ram – to secure justice and dignity for their communities. I visited Dalit temples and *bhavans* in the UK. I learned that communities which I thought were well integrated with other Indian communities were not so. In order to make a contribution to fostering an understanding of their situation in the UK, the idea of a research project took shape. I am glad to say that my efforts have borne fruit and I hope that the findings of the project will make scholars and others undertake further research, and encourage social workers and teachers to initiate practical projects on this subject.

After five years researching the topic, I realize now my ignorance of the struggles, sacrifices, and nobility of the aforementioned Dalit leaders who fought sohard (as others are still doing) to claim their basic human rights. Thanks to their Herculean efforts, Mayawati was able to become Chief Minister of Uttar Pradesh (UP), India in 1995 – the first Dalit woman to hold such a position, and – again reached this position which she has occupied since 2006. Their heroic struggle is on a par with the leaders of other oppressed people such as Nelson Mandela and Dr Martin Luther King.

The New Constitution of India, formally adopted on 26 January 1950, outlawed untouchability and agued for affirmative action for Dalits, and in 2010 India proudly celebrated its sixtieth anniversary as a democratic Republic. The

Chairman of the Constitution Committee was Baba Sahib Dr Ambedkar, a Dalit, sometimes referred to as the father of the Constitution. His vision and ideas inspired future generations of Dalit leaders who have succeeded in their endeavours to make political and economic gains for their respective communities. However, much remains to be accomplished in this area. My own study makes a contribution to the social and educational aspects of Dalits in the UK.

In my view, all children and young people of Indian/South Asian origin (and indeed others) should benefit from studying the history and religious underpinning of the caste system. It should be a singular lesson in humanity and will teach them to be sensitive and caring individuals and to fight for social equality and the common good of all people.

Dalits, formerly called 'Untouchables', remain the most oppressed community in India (and indeed in South Asia), who, until recently, have been denied human and civic rights for almost two millennia. On emigration to the UK and other Western countries, they face a double disadvantage: caste discrimination from their fellow countrymen and racial discrimination from white society. Initially, the community remained invisible among visible South Asians, for three main reasons. First, it was to the advantage of first generation immigrants that they fuse their identities under the all encompassing Asian identity[1] (ascribed by Western host societies) to escape caste discrimination. Second, the community was not cohesive and united enough to assert its own identity. Third, there were very few educated and professional leaders who could energize and mobilize the whole community. However, in the late 1980s the second generation Dalit professionals emerged to challenge their low caste status and Brahmanism,[2] both in the West and in South Asia (Leslie, 2003; International Conference on Dalit Human Rights, 2000; Padmasuri, 1997). According to Caste Watch (2010), a Dalit organization in the UK, there are at least 50,000 Dalits in Britain, although estimates range as high as 200,000. An Indian-origin MP from Southall, London, asserts that caste-based thinking is built into the fabric of the estimated 3.5 million South Asians[3] living in Britain, constituting approximately 5.7 per cent of the population. He says it is not a Hindu issue but affects South Asian people of all religions (ACDA, 2010). There are over 166 million Dalits[4] in India and they constitute 16 per cent of the

---

1   In Britain people of Indian, Pakistani, and Bangladesh origin are called Asians, whilst in the US the term 'Asians' refers to people of Chinese, Vietnamese, and Korean origins. In this text I will use the term South Asians, except where my interviewees refer to Asians.

2   This implies caste superiority, snobbery, and exclusion.

3   Social and economic indicators across South Asia confirm that Dalits and other marginalized groups lack access to education, income, employment, health care, and land. A majority of Dalits live in extreme poverty and many are victims of forced or bonded labour (International Dalit Solidarity Network: Annual Report, 2005).

4   As noted earlier, Dalits are officially called Scheduled Castes, a term that dates back to the British Raj in 1934/35.

total population, but in some states, like the Punjab, their proportion is a great deal higher – nearly 29 per cent (Census of India, 2001).

The Untouchables of India have endured centuries of exclusion, humiliation, discrimination, and indeed dehumanization from high-caste people. Their situation was worse than that of African-Americans in the US until recent times (circa 1950s) because they were denied the basic human rights in their own country. They were not brought in as slaves from abroad but were free indigenous men and women (Ad Dharmis) who were subjected to degrading treatment for over two millennia.

There has been little research published on this community, or on their children's education, in the UK. Although caste organization and differentiation are to be found in the whole of South Asia, this book deals with Dalit communities who have emigrated from India. (Readers who are interested in the Pakistani Muslim Dalits and caste system are referred to the excellent Chapter 4 in Shaw's book (2000).) This research makes an original contribution by investigating problems and challenges facing Dalit communities who have settled in the UK, having immigrated in large numbers in the 1960s and 1970s along with their high-caste countrymen/women. Manusmriti (Olivelle, 2004), a classic Hindu law text, assigns them no place in the *Chaturvarna* (four castes) of society but places them outside the mainstream, which literally means they are 'outcaste', without any rights and privileges except to carry out the most degrading work of society. Their chores included the removal of dead animals, cleaning cowsheds and toilets, and sweeping roads. This was justified by invoking the twin concepts of karma and dharma. Karma implied that one's deeds in a previous life are responsible for one's present condition, *ergo* one should accept one's social position as a punishment or reward for previous bad or good deeds – a form of fatalism. Dharma[5] is a broad notion which implies one's duty, responsibility, obligation and so on to carry out one's caste occupational roles and prescribed duties. It was argued by caste Hindus that these 'outcastes' they are engaged in dirty and filthy work and become permanently polluted, they should be forced to live outside village boundaries. Surprisingly, a recent Report by Sharma (2008) published by the Hindu Council in the UK has offered a spirited defence of caste divisions on specious grounds. A detailed critique of the Report is given in the next chapter.

Gandhi (1927) called dharma, *swadharama*, and was of the view that caste divisions were, on the whole, for the benefit of society. However, he denounced untouchability and said it was against the spirit of Hindu holy texts such as the *Gita* and *Mahabharata*. Dalit leaders now condemn Gandhi as an apologist for the

---

5 The concept of dharma is the bedrock of the Hindu religion. The whole story of the *Ramayana* is based on this notion as is the epic of *Mahabharata*. In the narrative of the *Ramayana*, the young Lord Rama agrees to go into exile to fulfil his duty and obligation to his father. Likewise,s Arjuna agrees to fight his kith and kin in the story of the *Mahabharata* because Lord Krishna urges him to fulfil his dharma and fight a just war.

caste divisions. For example, Mayawati, the chief minister of *Uttar Pradesh* (UP), India, calls him a *nattick bazz*, a cheap dramatist.

In south India until the 1930s Dalits (Deliege, 1999) were not allowed to enter villages without prior warning, so that high-caste people could get out of their way; even their shadow was considered to be polluting. Hence the term *Achute* in Hindi – Untouchables – has been used both by Indians and foreigners.[6] Although the economic and social lives of Untouchables have improved through education, affirmative action, and their own political skills since the Independence of India in 1947, they still form the bottom layer of Indian society. The present situation is summarized by the distinguished historian, Bayly (1999: 368):

> Both under the British and in independent India, the Indian State has had a remarkable capacity to reinforce crucial elements of caste. This has occurred both through specific policies of social reform or caste-based 'uplift' … It has been, above all, the power of the pollution barrier that has been extended and reinforced in this way …

This is the structural view of a historian but the following more personal and subjective statement makes a similar point by an established anthropologist, Deliege (1999: 199):

> Untouchability persists, and one might even say that, from a certain point of view, it is thriving in spite of modern ideologies. All one has to do to be convinced of this is to talk with a high-caste peasant. One day an Udayar farmer in Tamil Nadu told me a story about a love affair similar to the one carried by *Times* magazine that I cited at the outset. There, too, the young people have been killed by the girl's father, and the father calmly explained that it was the only thing to do; he too would kill his children if they eloped with a Harijan (untouchable).

Deliege goes on to report that this sort of attitude is also to be found amongst the urban elite who consider themselves modern and progressive.

As noted above, Dalits, along with their other countrymen, immigrated to the UK and Western countries in the 1960s to seek their fortune. A retired man who was allowed to remain in the UK with his daughter expressed his feelings with exhilaration and joy:

> Every morning when I get up I salaam this country many times for providing me with accommodation, health care, and other amenities. In my Indian village I was treated as a piece of dirt. I would have perished … Here, I am respected

---

6   According to some scholars the term Untouchables was coined and first used by the British to designate all those who were shunned by high caste Hindus (Bayly, 1999).

as a person like any other high-caste person. It is a wonderful country. May
Bhagvan's [God's] blessing be showered upon it.

This book is based on extensive fieldwork and uses qualitative research
methodology, which includes in-depth interviews with parents, teachers, and
children, and detailed observations in *gurdwaras*, *bhavans*, homes, and schools
in Birmingham and the English West Midlands. A small-scale case study in
the Punjab was undertaken to broaden the research base and to give it a wider
meaning and perspective. The research was carried out over a period of five years
and extended formal and informal group discussions were important aspects of
data collection, as were the textual sources. In total, 104 students, teachers, school
governors and community leaders were interviewed (and many others were
interviewed informally). To obtain a broader perspective on the issues, samples
in the study also include high-caste people. Furthermore, the researcher attended
Dalit conferences and meetings to observe and discuss matters relating to the
main themes of the book. The main perspective of the narrative is embedded
within social psychology but perspectives and insights from other disciplines (for
example, anthropology and sociology) also form an important part of the story.

The book pursues three interrelated themes: the reproduction of caste and its
awareness among Indian immigrants in the UK; the role of religious institutions
and other agencies in perpetuating caste consciousness; and the role of education
and Dalit-led initiatives in counteracting the negative affects of caste prejudice
and discrimination.

Chapter 2 gives a brief history of caste organization and differentiation in
India since the times of Manu circa first century BCE.[7] It traces the challenges
mounted by the Buddha and his followers to Brahmanism. Gautama Buddha
reinterpreted the concept of karma (which is the lynchpin of the caste system)
by stressing the agency of human beings and their free will. He admitted into his
sanga both Untouchables and women. The next serious challenge was mounted by
saints of the Bhakti movement (twelfth-mid-eighteenth century CE)[8] who argued
that we are all born of 'One Divine Light' and that anyone can achieve nirvana
irrespective of their caste, creed, or gender. To achieve nirvana one does not need
not to go through purification rituals, pilgrimages to holy places, and personal and
animal sacrifices. Devotion to God with all one's heart is what is required. Bhagat
Kabir and Guru Ravidas Ji were the movements most popular protagonists. Sikh
gurus also followed this aspect of the Bhakti movement and denounced caste
and gender discrimination, but their followers have generally retained Hindu
caste divisions. Indeed, caste differentiation has been the source of bitter division
within Sikh communities in the UK, Europe and North America. We refer to

---

7   'Manu became the symbol of oppression. His verses were cited as the source of
legitimation for such oppression' (Olivelle, 2004: xvii).

8   Bhakti emphasizes the intense emotional attachment and love of a devotee toward
his personal God (British Encyclopedia, 2004).

this matter frequently in the text. The chapter concludes with a discussion of the highly significant contribution of Dr Ambedkar to the Dalit cause and presents an up-to-date picture of the Dalits' political success in terms of the historic election of Ms. Mayawati (a Dalit) to the position of Chief Minister of Uttar Pradesh, the most populous state of India. This event is of course not as momentous as the election of Barack Obama in the USA; nevertheless it is an extremely significant step in building up both the Dalit image and Dalit confidence in India and abroad.

Chapter 3 sets the scene for the empirical work of the book and presents the social and economic backgrounds of a Dalit community in a Punjabi village. It aims to assist the reader in appreciating the challenges that Dalits face in the UK. It is a case study of one village and traces the socio-economic developments that have come about since Indian independence in 1947. It offers an analysis of the sea changes that have taken place in a village in the domain of social relationships and social interchange, the treatment of women, mixed residential housing, control of the village panchayat (council), and economic independence. The chapter highlights the agents of that change, namely: education, economic independence, the emergence of a Dalit middle class, and the support of civil authority for equality and social justice, and numerical strength. The change in schooling and education of village children over a period of 50 years is also tackled in Chapter 3.

Chapter 4 focuses on the religious, social, and family organizations of Dalits in the English Midlands. It is based on the extensive aforementioned fieldwork. The stress is on interviewees' perceptions and experiences and their voices gives ample space. Here emerges a fascinating story of Dalit communities who have actively built up their own religious and community places and thus provided a nurturing environment for their members and young people to feel comfortable with and even proud of their personal and social identities. But it is poignant that this has sharpened rather than blurred caste divisions within the Indian diaspora. This was perhaps bound to happen during the initial period of settlement abroad but lays the foundation for future inter-caste mixing and marriages on equal footings. Thus the chapter throws light on the cherished desire of many Dalits and other Indians that caste might whither away amongst the Indian diasporas in the UK and elsewhere in the West. Hence this chapter details one of the most salient topics of the book, namely, inter-caste mixing, and analyses the reaction of interviewees' to inter-caste marriages, caste awareness, and caste prejudice.

Chapter 5 is devoted to the education of Dalit young people. The focus is again on exploring caste-related issues. It describes the attitudes of young people towards caste awareness, inter-caste friendships, identities, school achievement, and their vocational aspirations. What emerges is a pleasing picture of young people making good progress on all fronts with the support of their teachers and parents. They are serious young people who are making the most of the opportunities offered and are acculturating into the norms of British society without losing their roots in Indian culture. Their views on caste-related matters are very balanced and well thought out and this should allay the anxieties of many parents who feel that their children might encounter serious problems in schools.[9]

It becomes clear from my observations that caste becomes an issue in schools where a majority of children are of Indian origin. Consequently Chapter 6 deals with a range of educational and caste-related matters from the teachers' perspective. Teachers' perceptions and attitudes are crucial in nurturing racial and caste harmony in multicultural schools. The fieldwork was conducted in two multicultural schools over a protracted period of time to observe and interview both teachers and head teachers. The rich data is analysed and discussed in relation to the main strands of the book, namely caste awareness and reproduction, and policies to counteract the negative impact of caste differentiation. I was struck by the openness, honesty, and integrity of the interviewees who took the subject seriously and gave reflective answers to our queries. This chapter also discusses the views of parents on their children's education. It notes that most parents in the study are satisfied with the schooling and education of their young people in British schools. They value education highly and are keen to give the best opportunities to their young people. Their views on caste are fully explored.

The final chapter returns to the main theme of the book and links together the findings of the empirical research. It presents a picture of Indian Dalit communities in the UK by knitting together the present findings and the existing literature on the subject and suggests educational policies that can be productive in tackling caste issues. Research into Dalit communities in the UK is sparse and I think this is due to the lack of knowledge on the topic and its significance. Social and educational research is needed to inform teachers and others of the importance of caste-related matters amongst people of Indian/ South Asian origins in the UK and elsewhere.

Scores of people were interviewed for this research and in Appendix A, six case studies are presented in order to give the reader vivid scenarios of Dalit people's lives and the challenges they have faced or are facing in the UK and India. The selection was based on the fact that I managed to maintain contact with these people over a protracted period of time and had opportunities to contact them again for clarifications and amendments.

---

9   However, according to a recent report by ACDA (2010) quite a number of students do encounter caste name-calling and bullying.

Chapter 2
Origin and Theories of the Caste System

Introduction

Indian caste stratification is unique in the world in that its structure, organization, and perpetuation, despite many changes, have endured for over two millennia. There are regional (north and south) variations as well as rural and urban differences, but caste in its manifold versions survives in India. It affects the Indian people's whole way of life, although religious affiliation, for example, to Sikhism and Islam, may soften its impact. Its effect on people's lives is profound: from the rites of passage through to social and inter-personal relationships, to religion, politics, and economic matters. There are a number of theories, which explain the origin and working of this social system and we shall examine them in the following sections.

We start our discussion with the concept of social class, which is widely understood in Europe and North America. Social class is the result of the stratification of members of a society based on their occupation (that is, division of labour) and life style. Thus in British society (leaving aside the Royalty and very wealthy landed gentry) there are broadly speaking three classes: upper class, middle class, and working class. The upper class consists of people with extensive power and wealth who occupy such prestigious jobs as cabinet ministers, senior civil servants, owners of factories and businesses. The middle class is mainly composed of professionals and semi-professionals and includes doctors, solicitors, engineers, and university and school teachers. Finally the working class comprises skilled or semi-skilled workers, and manual workers. These occupational positions are achieved through education and are open to all members of society irrespective of their parents' religion or occupation. Thus, there is social mobility between the classes, however limited it may be in practice.

According to some theorists (Deliege, 1999; Weber, 1958), the origin of the caste system was originally akin to the class system but became rigid and ossified due to the exploitation by the upper classes of the lower orders. Thus, in the distant past Brahmins, Kshatriya, and Vaishya, the three high castes, who held most of the economic resources, exploited the labouring classes, which included leather-tanners, and people who removed human and animal wastes. With the passage of time, those carrying out dirty and menial work were deemed to be unclean and were excluded from mainstream society. Another caste (Shudra) was added to the system to serve the three high castes. Thus came into existence the concept of *Chaturvarna* (four *varnas*). Although reference to *varna* is to be found in the sacred scriptures of Hindus (*Rig Vedas*) and the *Dharamsastra*, Manu[1] (circa first century BCE and the second century ACE, Olivelle, 2004: xxiii) added religious legitimacy to the system by specifying the rites, purity rituals, and duties associated with each caste. He also described in detail the penalties for transgressing caste boundaries, especially inter-caste marriages and social interactions.

Religious Interpretation of Caste

The four *varna* consisted of Brahmins (priests), Kshatriya (fighters and rulers), Vaisya (farmers and cattle keepers), and Shudra[2] (artisans such as blacksmiths, weavers, and potters), and finally at the bottom of the hierarchy and outside the *Chaturvarna* (four castes) were placed people who were assigned menial and degrading jobs as noted above. They were called *Candala*[3] whose mere touch would defile and pollute people of high castes. Manu's[4] authoritative and legalistic book had a great influence on the psyche of Hindus. Olivelle (2004: 183) interprets Manu's thinking on the plight of Untouchables:[5]

> Candalas and Svapacas (that is, Untouchables), however, must live outside the village ... their property consists of dogs and donkeys, their garments are the clothes of the dead; they eat in broken vessels; their ornaments are of iron; and they constantly roam about ... A man who follows the law should never seek any dealings with them. They depend on others for their food, and it should

---

1   The eponym 'Manu', of course, is not the name of the historical author of this text ... Manu was regarded not just as the first human being but, at least according to one tradition, as the first king (Olivelle, 2004: xxi).

2   Also spelt Sudra (*OED*).

3   Sometimes written as *Chandala*, a name given to *Achutes* – Untouchables.

4   Olivelle (2004) uses 'Manu' as a shorthand term for the historical author of the law code.

5   Most of the basic ideology on *varna* theory and its relation to *karma*, *dharma*, *guna*, and other broad principles mentioned in the preceding pages still persists in the mind of the average Hindu (Pandarinth, 1993: 321). A classic book by Pandharinth (1943) deals with the caste system and other aspects of Hindu social organization. It has gone through several reprints and appears to be widely used by scholars in India and abroad. The author argues that although the *varna* system was established in ancient times – as references to it are found in the *Mahabharata* and the Rig Veda – the four varans form the bedrock of Indian village society even now, that is, 1993. He reluctantly admits that there is another caste, viz., the Untouchables, but this is mentioned only once in his 150-page long chapter (284–335). It is implied that this is a recent addition; but they were considered outside the caste system by the writer of the *Manusmiriti*. It is clear from his arguments that he is also treating the Untouchables as 'invisible' people who are born to carry out the most menial tasks of the society, and they are not part of the Hindu civic society.

be given in a broken vessel. They must not go about in villages and towns at night …

The notion of purity and impurity is central to the understanding and theorizing of the Hindu caste system according to Dumont (2004). From his interpretation of Hindu scriptures such as the Vedas and *Manusmriti* Dumont argues that in the bipolar dimension of purity and impurity Brahmins are at one end of the spectrum and Untouchables at the other. Brahmins were to engage in religious and priestly concerns, the teaching of holy scriptures, and to perform the correct rituals and rites on auspicious occasions. The Untouchables were to carry out the most menial and degrading work of society and to eat the leftovers of the upper castes as noted earlier. Such degrading work was supposed to pollute people in body, mind, and spirit and thus they were to be excluded from civic society and confined to enclaves outside villages. Furthermore, it is argued in *Manusmriti* that their birth into untouchable families is due to evil and sinful deeds (karmas) committed in past lives. It is the Untouchables' karma (fate) that has determined their present social positions and they should serve mainstream society by adhering to their *dharma*[6] (religious duty) and serving others from a position of humility. Thus, the twin concepts of *karma* and *dharma* supported the caste system and in time these notions became the cornerstone of Hindu philosophy and way of life. At a village level the way the caste system worked was through several sub-castes known as *jatis*. This is defined by Srinivas (2002: 199): 'Another grey area in our understanding of caste is the manner in which the jati system[7] emerged and spread all over the country, jati being a local hereditary, and endogamous unit practicing a traditional occupation, frequently along with agriculture (landowner, tenant or labourer) and some form of trade.' *Jati* hierarchy is the same as that of the caste: Brahmins at the top and Untouchables (now called Dalits) at the bottom.

---

6 According to Brown (1988: 169) 'There is no single English word which embraces the concept of dharma. It is your essential nature, law, duty, and path.' The concept of *dharma* is extensively used in the story of the *Ramayana* to justify and explain the life and activities of Lord Rama (see 2000). In the *Mahabharata* the sermon given by Lord Krishna to Arjuna is based on *dharma*. *Dharma* is the basis of the Hindu social order (Pandharinath, 1993: 357).

7 The *varna* system as described here is an abstracted schema constructed from Shastras during the Vedic time (see Dumont 2004). The way caste system is played out in Indian villages, however, is through a plethora of *jatis* (sub-castes) which are endogamous. Although Brahmins are deemed to be at the top of the purity impurity continuum and caste hierarchy, they may not always be a dominant force in a village, according to Srinivas (2002: 1999). Furthermore, the so-called lower castes of Vaishya and Shudra may become Kshatriya over a period of time through conquest and/or economic dominance. Thus in practice there has been some cast mobility both at a corporate and individual level, especially during the pre-British time (see Srinivasa, 2002). Nevertheless, the caste status of Untouchables who are outside the *varna* system has remained static.

The vast majority of Indian people during the ancient times internalized this philosophy and accepted their social positions, until it was challenged by Gautama Buddha[8] (c. 624–544 BCE). Before describing Buddhist philosophy and its impact on the caste system, we summarize the basic tenets of caste which are also referred to as *varna* and at a village level *jati*. Firstly, caste is determined by birth and therefore no attempt should be made to change one's position. Secondly, endogamy is an important aspect of the caste system and inter-caste marriages are forbidden. Thirdly, the pollution barrier stipulates that Untouchables should remain outside the civic society. Lastly, people should live according to their caste rituals and rites and thereby fulfil their religious duty and obligations, that is, *dharma*, by staying within their caste folds. It is also important to note that within the four caste divisions there are literally dozens of subdivisions called jatis. Thus in a typical Punjabi village 50 years ago there were *jhirs* (water carrier), *nai* (barbers), *tharkhans* (carpenters), *julias* (weavers), *lohars* (blacksmiths) all belonging to the Shudra caste – the lowest rung in the four-fold caste hierarchy.

A vivid description of an Untouchable's role even in a modern-day Indian village is given by Burra (1996: 153):

> Amongst the functions of a Mahar doing *gaonki* were cutting wood for the villagers, taking wood to the cremation ground, taking messages of birth and death, accompanying marriage party ..., removing dead cattle from houses and cleaning wells ... The socioeconomic status of the Mahars was extremely low. Their touch was defiling and they lived isolated in the *mharwada*, always separated from the living areas of the caste Hindus

Challenge of Buddhism

The Buddha's religious philosophy is wide ranging and an in-depth treatment of its tenets would be a diversion from the main thesis of the book (details are to be found elsewhere: see Gombrich, 1988; Klostermaier, 1999; Omvedt, 2003). What concerns us here is the challenge which Buddhism posed to Brahmanism and its perspective on caste. All human beings share the same predicament of living and face the problem of *dukh* (suffering), according to the basic tenet of the Buddha. To alleviate suffering the Buddha enunciated the eight-fold path to salvation.[9] Further, principles of non-violence, mindfulness, and living in harmony with the world were also a refreshing antidote to the Brahmans' view of the world in which caste hierarchy and rank prevailed. Keer (2005: 466) argues that the Buddha rejuvenated and reorganized the social and religious systems of the

---

8   The Buddha's exact date of birth and death are controversial (see Omvedt, 2003: 23).

9   The eight-fold path is: right speech, right conduct, right thinking, right mindfulness, right livelihood, right aspirations, right effort, and right views (Klostermaier, 1999: 35).

Hindus by denouncing the ritual sacrifices and priesthood/priest craft of Brahmins and laid stress on the individual's own effort to achieve nirvana. Klostermaier (1999: 56) writes: 'Contrary to Brahmanism of his time, the Buddha taught the essential equality of the possibilities for liberation available to all, regardless of gender, race or caste … there is nothing in the basic teaching that is gender specific.' According to Ambedkar, the Buddha, by admitting women to the life of *parivrajka* (an ascetic), gave them the right to knowledge and the right to realize their spiritual potentialities along with men (Keer, 2005: 428). The Buddha preached the value of self-reflection and meditation rather than engaging in caste-related rituals to achieve salvation (*nirvana/nibana*). Even Buddhism's stance on the transmigration of souls and the omnipresence of God was muted. All human beings can achieve *nirvana/nibana* irrespective of their caste, rank, or gender. The aim in life is to reduce/overcome *dukh* (suffering) and this objective is best pursued through *madhym marg* – the middle path. This involved practising right views, right speech, right actions, right behaviour, and right thinking and was open to all to develop their spirituality. Gombrich (1988: 6–7), a distinguished scholar of Buddhism, writes: 'A crucially important instance of the previous idea, that life is a process, is the law of *karma*. This states that all sentient beings are ethical agents. They have the power to decide whether to do good or ill, but this power is curtailed in that they are influenced by their own previous decisions.' This notion of *karma* is different from the one commonly understood and practised by Hindus of predestination and suffering, which is encapsulated in a remark uttered by many Hindus: 'It was my *karma* that I have met this misfortune and suffering.' The Buddha stressed the importance of free will and one's own efforts to make one's own *karma* in this life.

The real flowering of Buddhism took place during Asoka's reign (c. 274–236 BCE) who adopted it both at a personal and a state level and preached its message in India and abroad by dispatching priests (called *bhikshus*), and erecting monuments and statues in honour of the Buddha.

According to Klostermaier (1999: 56), Buddhism flourished for about a thousand years after its inception but under the patronage of the Gupta dynasty (circa 500 ACE) Brahmins launched a counterattack and eventually Hinduism again became a dominant religion. Singh (1999: 19), a distinguished historian, concurs with this assessment: 'At the birth of Christ for seven hundred years or more, the predominant faith of India was Buddhism.' It was not until the twelfth century that saints and reformers belonging to the Bhakti movement mounted another substantial challenge to caste organization.

Bhakti Movement (Medieval Period – circa Twelfth to Mid-Eighteenth Century)

The founder of this movement was Ramanuja (circa 1016–1137) who was born in South India but travelled throughout north India preaching his new found religious insights. The basic principles included: there is one God, and the best way to serve God is total submission to his will, and by the chanting of mantras. This could best be achieved under the guidance of a spiritual leader, that is, guru, and this way of worship is open to all irrespective of caste or creed.

Low-caste and Untouchable people, who were completely excluded from worshipping in Hindu temples produced saints/poets who were inspired by the above message to challenge the hegemony of Brahmins. They were also partly influenced by Islamic beliefs, forbidding idol worship and believing in one God (Allah). The most famous saints of this movement include, Kabir, Namdev, Ravidas, and Dhanna. They believed (and preached) in the equality of all humankind and attacked the very notion of caste. Kabir's hymns poignantly sum up their philosophy.

Kabir writes (Hess, 1983: 19):

> Pandit (Brahmin), look in your heart for knowledge
> Tell me where untouchability
> Came from, since you believe in it.
> We eat by touching,
> we wash by touching, from a touch
> the world was born.
> So who's untouched? Asks Kabir
> Only he
> Who has no taint of Maya.
> And
> Its all one skin and bone
> One piss and shit
> One blood, one meat
> From one drop, a universe.
> Who's Brahmin? Who's Shudra?

Likewise, Guru Ravidas who was born in an untouchable Chamar family in Benares (Varanasi), the holy city of Hindus, challenged Brahmins to demonstrate their purity vis-à-vis the impurity of the lower castes. There are many legends popular among his devotees which bear out his divine birth and the miracles he performed in the name of *Har* ('one God') to falsify the Brahmin's claim to purity and exclusive right to salvation. Brahmins disingenuously accepted the story of his low birth but attributed it to his bad *karma* and argued that he was redeemed for his good deeds in this life. Guru Ravidas is revered mostly by Chamars (traditionally leather workers) and there are a large number of temples founded in his name in the UK, Europe, and North America.

Srinivas (1996: xv), a renowned Indian scholar of caste, sums up the Bhakti movement:

It was a powerful movement which surfaced in various parts of the sub-continent over several centuries. It was anti-caste, pro-poor, pro-women, anti-elitist, anti-Sanskrit, and it affirmed that genuine love of god was sufficient to achieve salvation … The Bhakti movement attracted large numbers of the lower castes, and the poor and lowly, including women.

Sikhs and Untouchables

Guru Nanak Dev (1469–1539), founder of Sikh religion, was greatly influenced by the Bhakti movement and pronounced his faith in one Creator (*Ek ung Oankar*), who is omnipotent, truthful, and without fear and omnipresent. *Ek noor te sub jagat upja kon bale kon mande* (we are the product of one divine light and who is to judge who is good and who is bad)? He advocated equal rights for women. His famous saying is: 'Women who give us birth, nurture and sustain us should be honoured and not exploited. It is the ignorant who treat them badly.' His way to salvation is through pious living, hard work, and devotion to one God. He challenged Brahmins on their empty rituals and superstitious rites and sacrifices. His nine successors further developed his basic teaching to overcome the caste system and to forge a common *panth* (movement) against tyranny and the injustice of their contemporary Mughal rulers. The notable features of this developed religion included: eating together in a communal *langar* (kitchen); all men followers were to have the surname Singh (lion) and women Kaur (princess); and all who partake baptism become *Khalsa* (pure) irrespective of their caste and gender. It follows that Sikh religion should be free of caste consciousness and discrimination. Sikh scholar Duggal (1988: 34) describes Sikh principles:

> The anointed Sikh was not to smoke or take any other intoxicants. He must be loyal to his spouse and not covet other women. All Sikhs were equal; there was no high or low caste among Khalsa. The Khalsa believed in one god … and must help the needy and protect the poor. The Sikhs who adopt the prescribed way of life are as good as the Guru. The guru is the Khalsa and the Khalsa is the Guru.

However, these noble principles have not been completely upheld by Sikhs and caste has never lost its hold on the majority of Hindu converts to the new religion. Valmikis who converted to Sikhism were not fully accepted and are called *mazhabi* Singhs and likewise when Chamars converted they came to be known as Ravidasi Singh. Living proof of this is also to be found now in the UK and elsewhere where *gurdwaras* are caste based, ergo: Jats, *tharkhans*, *bhatras*, Chamars, and so on (see Kalsi, 1992).

At this point it is important for the reader to note that those who converted to Islam and Christianity, especially high caste Hindus (for example, Rajputs) retained their caste affiliations and continued to enjoy their privileges. Untouchables who embraced Islam and Christianity, likewise, continued to suffer the same indignities as they did within the folds of Hinduism (Bhatty, 1976; Tharamangalam, 1996). Srinivas (1996: xxxiv) sums it up succinctly: 'The fact that caste continues to characterize Indian Islam and Christianity means that the dogma of the equality of all members of each religion has not been strong enough to dissolve it.'

Mahatma Gandhi and Untouchables (circa 1920–1948)

Gandhi, father of the nation, was an extremely influential figure in the Indian freedom movement and in his attempts to improve the dire conditions of the Untouchables. He called them Harijans (children of God) to purge Hinduism of its taboos and inhuman practices associated with untouchability. The newly coined label became an accepted and politically correct term in describing the predicament of oppressed people, until it was challenged by Ambedkar (see the following section), who thought the new name was patronizing and condescending. Gandhi made a point of residing in *bhangi* (Untouchables) colonies during his travels preaching his message of *ahimsa* (non-violence) and *satyagraha* to mobilize support for Indian independence. He cleaned his own toilets and made his wife do the same despite her vehement objections (Gandhi, 1927). He established the *satyagraha* ashram at Allahabad and admitted a Dalit family to its membership. In his own words, he describes this experience:

> But their admission created a flutter amongst the friends who had been helping the ashram ... The man in charge of the water lift objected that drops of water from our bucket would pollute him. So he took to swearing at us and molesting Dudabhia ... All monetary help, however, was stopped.

Despite all these problems Gandhi and his ashram companions persevered and set an example to his followers and others that untouchability is not part of their creed. Within the Congress Party he was instrumental in setting up a special movement (All India Suppressed Classes Federation) for ameliorating the very poor economic and social conditions of Dalits.

However, he justified the *varna* system by invoking Hindu holy scriptures and also the necessity for specializations of occupational skills. For instance, he argued that a carpenter becomes a master carpenter if his ancestors have followed the same pursuit because of his heredity and socialization into the mores and ways of carpentry right from childhood.[10] But Gandhi strongly denied that untouchability

---

10   Pandharinath (1993) endorses such a perspective on caste and even suggests that the Untouchables are a recent addition to the caste system (Chapter 8 on Four Varnas: 234–85).

is part of the Hindu *varna*. Zelliot (1972: 73) quotes from Gandhi's writing:[11] 'The law of *varna* prescribes that a person should, for his living, follow the lawful occupation of his forefathers, but with the understanding that all occupations are equally honorable: a scavenger has the same status as a Brahmin.' Equating society to a *pursa* (person), he says that a *pursa*'s feet (that is, Shudras – low castes) are as important as his head (representing high-caste Brahmins). It cannot be merely coincidence that a Hindu organization in the UK justifies the caste system by using the same argument (see Pandit Sharma,[12] 2008). Gandhi's analysis is that untouchability crept into the system later on due to the misinterpretation of holy texts. However, those who have researched this matter think that Gandhi was an apologist for the caste system (Joshi, 1982). Furthermore, such a pious hope of equality of castes and *jatis* could never be realized in practice, as students of social class would readily appreciate. Radical Untouchable leaders of the time (1920–1940) observed that Gandhi's main aim was to unite and mobilize Hindus to gain independence from the British, whereas their chief aim was to throw away the yoke of *varna* and fight for equality with high castes.

Presently, the leader of the BJS (Bahujan Samaj Party), Mayawati, has dismissed Gandhi's contribution to the uplift of Dalits as derisory and cynically called his attempts cheap dramatics (*natticks*). In folk plays and mock judicial trials in UP, where Mayawati is Chief Minister, Gandhi and Manu are hanged because of their evil deeds perpetrated on the Untouchables (Narayan, 2006: 213).

British Raj and the Caste System

The British Raj in India lasted for nearly 300 years and left its legacy and mark on Indian political and social institutions and way of life. After the Mutiny revolt of 1857 and the takeover of administration by the British Crown many Indians had strong faith in the British Empire. This included stalwart leaders of the Indian freedom movement such as Gandhi and Nehru who until the early twentieth century thought the Raj was to herald a new era of 'science and technology' and social reform. Many Indians subscribed to the view held by a grandfather whom I interviewed in a village:

> English rule did bring law and order and non-corrupt government. A woman could wear jewellery and walk alone from one end of the Punjab to the other and she won't be molested ... They built canals for irrigation and brought prosperity to farmers and others ... They are very disciplined and hard working quom.

---

11   *Young India*, 17 November, 1927. Zelliot's (1972) article is an excellent source of insight into Gandhi's views on caste. In my view, though, Zelliot's analysis shows contradiction in Gandhi's perspective on the Hindu *varna* system. Gandhi was an idealist who wanted social reality to be as desired rather than as it is or has been.

12   Sharma has chosen the title Pandit to show that he is a high-caste Brahmin.

This grand old man (aged 90 years) had heard stories from his grandmother of social chaos and the breakdown of law and order after the break up of the Sikh Raj in the 1840s (see Singh, 1999) following the death of Maharaja Ranjit Singh and eulogized the benefits of the British rule.

Those who were opposed to the Raj argued that advantages bestowed on the country such as the railways, the legal system, the English language, and scientific education were the byproducts of the mechanisms of governance and political control. Their perspective was that colonization was about economic exploitation under the cloak of many feeble rationales such as spreading 'Western civilization', and a scientific and secular outlook.

Some Dalit leaders have argued (see Mangoo Ram in this chapter) that the British Raj tried to minimize the pernicious affect of the caste system by introducing equity in administration and employment, but it was too entrenched in the Hindu psyche to make much difference. Even the conversion of Untouchables to Christianity did not alter the situation because prejudice and discrimination were carried over, and nor did efforts by other institutions such as the Armed forces and the railways dent caste divisions and prejudice.

There are scholars (Said, 1995; Sharma, 2008) who argue that the British, intentionally or unintentionally, strengthened and reinforced the caste system rather than weakening it. The Indian caste system came very close to the rigid British class system of the time and provided a template for understanding Indian society. However, Bayly (1999: 373) argues that it was not a British invention or fabrication, but that 'this stereotyping, classifying, and essentializing' was adapted directly from the previous Hindu and Muslim rulers. Bayly goes on to say 'After mid-century [nineteenth], caste became one of the main categories of enumeration in an enormous array of official and quasi-official reportage, most notably in the decennial Census as well in the writings and operations of missionaries, medics, jurists, land settlement officers, military recruiters ... . '

The census data provided a good schema to designate some castes (Rajputs, Dogras) and quoms (Sikhs) as martial and they consequently became the backbone of the British Army. Other castes, like Chamars and Valmikis, were designated as serving classes and were not allowed to buy land to farm because that was not their ancestral occupation. Bayly (1999: 126) writes: 'By the of the end of [nineteenth] century an array of official materials including military recruitment manuals, gazetteers and Census reports featured listings assigning people of particular title and background to a certain order or status ("ruling" or "military" caste for example, as opposed to "scavengers" and "lower village menials"), with honourable or ignominious qualities being imputed to each group.' And on page 371 the author states: 'The experience of untouchability as a widely shared "disability" of large numbers of labouring, artisanal and service people was in many ways a real, if unintentional, creation of British rule.' Thus it seems that Untouchables became even more entrenched in their lowly status and servitude. Thereafter caste was used to divide Indian leaders and population. The split between Gandhi and Ambedkar in the 1930s is a good example of the schism created by emphasis on separate 'caste representation' for legislatures. It seems that the British were keen to see that the Untouchables did not join the national freedom movement lead by the Congress under the guidance of Gandhi. It is clear from historical records (Misra, 2007) that the British did not contemplate any serious social reform after the Mutiny Revolt of 1857, as it was believed that revolt was triggered by the widespread rumours amongst the sepoys that their faiths were being interfered with by the ruling British East India Company. Therefore, it is not unreasonable to conclude that the British used caste (just as they used religion and the native maharajas) as another dimension to deepen existing tensions and disunity amongst Indians in the hope of prolonging their rule.

There is another perspective on the controversy. According to Hobson (2010 website), a rationale for holding and maintaining the large Empire had to be devised. This came from the newly emerged discipline of anthropology and population statistics. Anthropology at that time was very Eurocentric and provided justification for the hierarchy of races (European on the top and Negro at the bottom of the ladder and other colonials somewhere in the middle) making it easy to extrapolate an understanding of the caste system in India.

Hobson (2010: 18) concludes his essay: 'For the Indian people, the census acted as a catalyst for an increased consciousness of caste as caste became an increasingly significant factor in attaining material status.'

Indian Reformers during the British Raj

Hindu liberal thinkers, notably Swami Dayanand Sarsawati and Rabindranath, Tagore, made strenuous efforts to reform Hinduism from the mid-nineteenth century onwards (Keane, 2007). The former founded Araya Samaj which argued that the caste system and untouchability as practised is not in consonance with Hindu Holy Scriptures. The Samaj argued that no body should be barred from reading the *Vedas* and *Gita* and worshipping in temples by virtue of their birth. People can achieve the highest caste rank by following the virtuous path and Hindu code of conduct. Other reforms of Hindu practices included: the prohibition of child marriage and *sati*; reform of the treatment of widows; and forbidding idol worship in temples. They also initiated a ceremony called *Shudi* (purity) in which Untouchables who had embraced Islam and Christianity were reconverted to the Hindu fold. Arya Samaj also made a great impact in north India by opening schools, colleges, and other institutions of learning and extending educational opportunities to all irrespective of caste. However, the overall caste framework was not challenged, except for the upward mobility of the lower castes. Vivekananda (1989: 245–6), another reformer, however, was a supporter of the caste divisions, though he condemned the poor treatment of the Untouchables. He writes:

> Look at the apple. The best specimens have been produced by crossing, but once crossed, we tried to keep that variety intact ... Caste is a natural order; I can

perform one duty in social life and you another; you can govern a country and I can mend a pair of old shoes, but that is no reason why you are greater than I ... Caste is good. That is the only natural way of solving life's problems.

In an ideal world this may be deemed to be true but in real life status depends upon, among other things, one's economic resources, level of education, tradition, and life style. Such pious and idealistic thinking was a hallmark of many Indian social reformers of the time, including Gandhi, who thought the Hindu *varna* (caste system) had united India against foreign invasions and is quintessentially a Hindu moral and spiritual order.

Baba Sahib Ambedkar (1892–1956)

The doctrine of past karma is purely Brahminc doctrine. Past karma taking effect in present life is quite consistent with Brahminc doctrine of soul, the effect of karma on soul. But it is quite inconsistent with the Buddhist doctrine of non-soul ... it has been bodily introduced into Buddhism by someone who wanted to make Buddhism akin to Hinduism or who did not know what the Buddhist doctrine was (Ambedkar, 1997: 343).

Dr Ambedkar is treated almost as a deity by many of his followers because of his total dedication, achievements, and sacrifice in the cause of Dalits. His interpretation of the Buddhist basic notion of *karma* is original and is radically different from that of established understanding, but it is accepted as authentic and progressive by his followers. He argues that the Buddha would have never defined *karma* as 'predestination' as he stipulates that environment is more important than heredity. There is some support for his views from the distinguished scholar, Gombrich (2006: 68–73), explains that if karma is located in the mind, all sentient beings are ethically on the same footing. In particular, the caste-bound ethic of Brahmanism is denied, since intention is the same whether it is intended by male or female, young or old, Brahmin or outcaste. He goes on: 'Karma is all-important, but by this is meant what you, the agent, decide to do. Here karma doctrine is an assertion of free will.'

Ambedkar sought inspiration and guidance from the Buddha's teachings to redress the huge injustices and cruelty meted out to his people. According to his biographer, Keer (2005: 524):

He was son of the 'dust.' He came of the family whose hundred forefathers were treated in this land worse than dogs, whose touch was regarded as pollution and whose shadow a sacrilege.

Words like devotees, master, deity are used by his biographer, showing the deep reverence in which Ambedkar is held by his followers.[13] For instance, his statue is in close proximity to that of the Buddha in Indian Buddhist temples and abroad. Their salutation is '*Jai Bhim*' (victory to Ambedkar). There is no doubt that he was one of the great leaders of the oppressed, and indeed of all Indians, whose contribution to the cause and uplift of Dalits is similar to that of Dr Martin Luther King to the African Americans in the US and of Nelson Mandela to black South Africans.

Dr Ambedkar was born in a low-caste family of Mahar (similar to Chamars of the Punjab) in Maharashtra in 1891, but because of his father's position in the British Army he enjoyed good schooling and graduated from Bombay University in 1912. With the financial help of the local maharaja he went to study in the US and England and earned two doctorates and also qualified as a barrister. He was a diligent and very bright student who won several awards and the fulsome praise of his professors. On returning to India in 1917, he met an appalling level of entrenched caste abuse, prejudice, and discrimination, which was then widely prevalent against the Untouchables. He became politically active and championed the cause of his people for justice and equality and in so doing opposed Gandhi's views and policies. He argued that Gandhi's priority was to gain independence from the British whereas his was to free his own community from the enslavement of high-caste Hindus. He rejected Gandhi's outdated views on *varna* and wanted equal social, political, and economic opportunity for all.[14] He was accepted by the British as a genuine representative of the Untouchables at Gandhi's displeasure. This lead to a rift between the two political leaders, which was later resolved by a compromise (Poona Act 1935) in which Untouchables were given reservations (fixed number of seats) both at provincial and federal levels of legislature.

In his youth, Ambedkar was not overtly religious and believed that given full equality and justice untouchability would become outdated. In the 1920s he tried non-violent methods to seek entry to Hindu temples for his followers but his hopes were dashed when stalwart Hindus like Gandhi proposed a compromise on this central issue. Deliege (1999: 180) writes: 'The repeated failure of these

---

13   Lynch (1972: 97) argues that amongst Jatvas (Untouchables) of UP he is a prophet of Neo-Buddhism ... his deeds and virtues are constantly celebrated in verse and song; and whose picture, as a haloed Bodhisattva ... .

14   Zelliot (1972: 81) gives a flavour of Ambedkar's disagreement with Gandhi: 'However if one looks more closely one finds that there is a slight harmony ... for he does not insist on the removal of untouchability as much as he insists on the propagation of Khaddar (homespun cloth) or Hindu–Muslim unity. If he had he would have made the removal of untouchability a precondition of voting in the party. ... when one is spurned by everyone, even the sympathy shown by mahatma Gandhi is of no little importance ... . His scathing comment on Hindu scripture culminated in a public burning of *Manusmriti* in 1927, and in 1935 Ambedkar announced his vow to leave Hinduism entirely and to convert to some other religion ... Ambedkar thought Gandhi's idea of ennobling the scavenging profession as an outrage, a cruel joke.'

movements eventually convinced him, that the god sitting in the temple was made of stone.' Ambedkar then gave up his struggle to be part of Hinduism and vowed in 1935: 'I was born a Hindu but I will not die a Hindu.' He explored all other religions prevalent in India but opted for Buddhism, which he embraced in October 1956 only two months before his death. He chose Buddhism because it originated in India and its basic philosophy of alleviating suffering (*dukh*) was close to his own heart. The Buddha had low-caste individuals as his disciples and he was opposed to rituals and sacrifices as noted earlier in this chapter. It was a religion which preached against superstitions and stressed the importance of *prajana* (understanding and knowledge) and therefore rationality. Such attributes appealed to him and he commended it to his followers. Such was his appeal that approximately a quarter of a million of his people (Mahar) converted with him and another 100,000 after his death. His achievements are manifold. He was a law minister in the first post-Independence central government of India. He was chairman of the Constitutional Committee established to draw up the new constitution of India in 1948. He founded a Republican party whose successor is the BSP party which is now led by Mayawati (Dalit), Chief Minister of UP (Uttar Pradesh), the most populous state in India. She nurtures very high aspirations and aims to become Prime Minister of India one day.

Although he was not successful in uniting all the untouchable castes (Dalits) and mobilizing their support to challenge the Congress party's policies on the improvement and full liberation of his people, Ambedkar's ideas have radicalized and inspired generations of Dalits.[15] He is deified by his community of Mahar of Bombay (Mumbai) and his pictures and statues appear alongside Buddha and other Hindu deities in Untouchables' homes and temples. He was the first European-educated leader of the Dalits, urbane and sophisticated, who could engage with the then leaders of Congress and the British Government on an equal basis. His community is immensely proud of his achievements and he is a model for the contemporary leaders of Dalits and Other Backward Classes (low castes).[16]

Ad Dharam Movement Lead by Mangoo Ram (circa 1920–1965)

The fight for the human rights of Dalits in the Punjab goes back to the Ad Dharam movement of the 1920s, which came into existence along with similar movements in different parts of India. The goal of the movement was to forge a distinct identity for the Untouchables, independent of the established religions

---

15   Mendelsohn and Vicziany (1998: 217) assess Ambedkar in glowing terms: 'But despite the limitation of the Ambedkarite movement as an electoral and mobilizing force in western India, the thought and life of Babasaheb Ambedkar enjoy a tremendous and indeed fast growing potency across large parts of India.'

16   As explained earlier in the chapter, low castes are from the artisan class and are referred to as Other Backward Castes (see H.S. Verma, 2005).

for example, Hinduism and Sikhism. This transformation was to come through cultural renewals, spiritual regeneration, and political assertion, rather than seeking equality within the Hindu or Sikh fold. In my opinion, the Ad Dharam movement was substantially successful in fulfilling its objective.

Ad Dharam was founded in the Doab (Hoshiarpur and Jalandar districts) region of the Punjab and was lead, among others, by charismatic leader Mangoo Ram. After his high school education, during which he suffered numerous indignities (such as sitting outside the classroom for his lessons, teachers' cynicism and mockery) his well-off father, who owned a leather business, sent him to the US to expand the family business. During his American sojourn, he mixed freely with people of all castes and religions and joined a revolutionary group (*ghadar*) to overthrow the British Raj. On his return to India, however, he was treated in the same demeaning way, as was the social custom of the time. This inspired him, along with his other colleagues, to found a new religion (Ram, 2004) in order to restore a sense of dignity, pride, and moral worth to the Untouchables. He argued that the Dalits were the original inhabitants of India (a somewhat contentious claim) and were conquered and subdued by Aryans – high-caste Hindus – from Iran. He claimed that our ancestors fought bravely but were defeated and received brutal treatment at the hands of the Aryans, and that we were excluded from the social world of the invaders and coerced into taking menial and degrading jobs. Here in his words expressed in the early 1930s the reader can appreciate his sentiments:

> We are the real inhabitants of this country and our religion is Ad Dharm. Hindu Quom came from outside to deprive us of our country and enslaved us … British rule should remain for ever. Make prayer before God. Except for this Government, no one is sympathetic towards us. Never consider ourselves as Hindus at all; remember that our religion is Ad Dharm (Ram, 1980: 290).

Such a clarion call had a great psychological impact on the Untouchables, though most of his followers were from his own community of Chamars. The tenets of Ad Dharam were never clearly stated but include: a belief in the teachings of Guru Ravidas and Sant Valmiki (also called Balmiki), the pursuit of truth, the equality of humankind, abstaining from intoxicants such as opium, bhang, and liquor, and a belief in the power of knowledge and education. Juergensmeyer (1982: 106) interprets it as follows:

> It's built upon a basis of early, perhaps aboriginal concepts of good and evil spirits and adds on traditions of formless god, the availability of spiritual power, distaste for dharmik Hinduism, and a respect for holy men and their spiritual practices. It had a vitality and coherence that marked it as a religious tradition of its own.

In a Punjabi village some Dalits may attend Sikh *gurdwaras* and also wear turbans and long hair and adhere to other emblems of Sikh traditions. Additionally, they may have a holy man called *siana* who guides them in marriage rituals, deaths, and other rites of passage. In addition, many seek spiritual solace in the world of nature by worshipping trees, *gogapir*, and ancestral shrines (see Chapter 3). It seems to me that Mangoo Ram and other the leaders of the Ad Dharam movement adopted the teachings of Guru Ravidas and other saints such as Kabir (noted above in section on Bhakti) to give their movement a deeper religious dimension in addition to linking their present situation to ancient historical roots. Thousands of Chamars and Bhangis in the Punjab embraced this religion and considered themselves on a par with Hindus, Muslims, and Sikhs.

In sum, many Untouchables of the Punjab have developed their own distinctive identity through Guru Ravidas ji's teaching and the Ad Dharam movement and feel confident in taking on the hegemony of Jats (the dominant farmer caste in Punjabi villages) as was witnessed in the events of May 2009 when militant Sikhs (allegedly) murdered one of their revered saints/gurus in a *gurdwara* in Austria and brought the whole of the Punjab to a standstill by rioting, burning, and marching in protest. One of the Dalits I interviewed gave me this response:

> We have to show 'them' that we are not going to be humiliated and treated as second class citizens any more. We can sacrifice our lives for our freedom [several of their people died in this turmoil]. We would practice our religion as we like and not what the Sikh establishment dictates.

More could be said on this matter, but here we note that the Ad Dharam movement inspired the Untouchables of Punjab to stand up for their rights and to make a bold political statement during the crisis.

In sum, the Ad Dharam movement has had a great deal of success in raising the morale and motivation of low-caste people but did not have a great deal of political success in the Punjab – its place of origin. It has inspired many future leaders of Dalits such as Kanshi Ram and Mayawati to carry on the fight for the uplift of Untouchable communities. Mangoo Ram sums up its achievements:

> Whatever rights we have now, it is because of the original Ad Dharam Mandal … During the British's rule, we were twice slaves: slaves of the British and slaves of the Hindus. We have got rid of the British, now we have to assert our own rights against the upper castes … We were inspired by Ravi Das, Kabir, and Nam Dev. Hinduism is a fraud on us. Ad Dharam is our only true religion (quoted in Juergensmeyer, 1982: 262).

It is worth noting again that Mangoo Ram fiercely disagreed with Gandhi's policies in his fight to uplift the dire conditions of his people. In the words of Juergensmeyer (1982: 130):

> Gandhi thought that the Ad Dharmis through their militant separatism were reinforcing the concept of caste divisions, and the Ad Dharmis thought Gandhi

was trying to whitewash existing differences in a superficial harmony. These are the differences that persist to the present day between Gandhians and militant Untouchables.

Contemporary Movements

A scholarly historical review of caste by Bayly (1999: 303) sums up the contemporary scene:

> The findings here are that clean-caste people generally regard all those whom they know to be of harijan/untouchable origin as permanently polluted and unclean in ritual terms, without any further differentiation between them.

Taking a cue from the above quote, we now describe the present situation of Dalits with special reference to Punjabis in the Punjab. Kanshi Ram (1934–2008) was one of the brightest and most astute followers of the Ad Dharam movement and was also inspired by the radical ideas of Ambedkar. He was originally from Hoshiarpur, Punjab, but chose to move to UP (United Provinces of India, before it was renamed Uttar Pradesh in 1950) to form a political party to succeed the Republican Party founded by Dr Ambedkar. It was to be called the BSP (Bahujan Samaj Party – majority common people's party) and its aim is to unite all the Untouchables, low castes, Muslims, and other dispossessed people to challenge the hegemony of the Congress government which had treated them as 'vote banks' since Independence in 1947. The late Kanshi Ram was described as fighting a holy war against the *Brahminwadi*, that is, against the Brahmin oppressors, and winning.

He was successful in his mission and formed an elected government in 1995, but the Chief Minister was Mayawati, a close associate of Kanshi Ram. According to some scholars (Mendelssohn and Vicziany, 1998), this was an historic occasion which inspired Dalits throughout India:

> But the very advent of such a Government has an electrifying effect across India. It was as if the world had been stood on its head, so that bottom ruled over the top. When Mayawati again came into power in April 1997 … the event was improbable without being unimaginable. The earlier accession had established.

Mayawati was elected again in 2007 and is the Chief Minister of UP, but her party (the BSP) did not maintain its momentum in the Lok Sabha (federal) election of 2009 due to several factors. Although she appealed widely to the poor, dispossessed, and Muslims, the votes were split amongst two other caste-based parties in the province. The Untouchables did not unite and this has been a major obstacle to their political and social progress now and in the past. As noted earlier, Dr Ambedkar made strenuous efforts to unify the Untouchable castes but failed to achieve his objective. However, despite these setbacks Mayawati – though somewhat controversial – has become a popular and charismatic leader who inspires the respect and adulation of her followers. Dalits have also made headway in politics at a national level in that they are no longer a vote bank for the Congress or any other national party but have built up their own parties.

Paradoxically though, Mayawati became Chief Minister with the help of the BJP (Bharatiya Janata Party) – a *Hinduvata* party which had advocated a traditional form of Hinduism in which *varna* plays an important role. Although the BSP party has had very little success in Punjab, Dalits in this province have shown how successfully they can make alliances with the Congress Party and Akali-Hindu[17] parties to their advantage rather than follow blindly the unique caste politics of UP.

Hindu Council UK Perspectives on Caste

> Historically, Varnashram has enabled Hindu civilization to survive repeated invasions. It has made Indian society stronger. It has served a purpose ... (Sharma, 2008: 3).

Sharma's 2008 report *The Caste System* was produced by the Hindu Council to counteract the charge of an 'evil and outmoded system' by various Dalit organizations (CasteWatch, 2010) and some European scholars (Deliege, 1999; Mendelsohn and Vicziany, 1998). The report is wide ranging in its coverage of caste issues and has many strands and themes which would require a great deal of space to critique. I will make some general points and then go on to address the central theme of the paper: the origin, nature and perpetuation of caste stratification and untouchability.

The document reads more like a polemical narrative than a carefully argued paper with supporting evidence to substantiate its claims. For example, on page 9 it says: 'Vedic scholars recognize ... ' but no scholars are cited. Again: 'Since Vedic times, caste has never been hereditary and in fact ... All Hindus, including those of low-birth [sic] and even unknown lineage, had the choice of pursuing any occupation, including that of a Brahmin.' The report[18] is replete with such statements with little empirical evidence or textual support.

The central theme of the report is that caste system was neither hereditary nor hierarchical, and that there was a fair degree of caste mobility. Furthermore, Shudras (low-caste people) were as important as the Brahmins because society is like a

---

17   Akali Party is mainly composed of Sikhs from the Punjab.

18   In his description of the caste system, Shudras (artisan class, barbers, carpenters) were created out of the feet of Pursha to serve the three high castes. But he does not mention the Untouchables who were not included in the four-*varna* system, but form nearly 17 per cent of the Indian population. Likewise, another noted scholar, Pandharinath (1993) only mentions the Untouchables as an afterthought when talking about the social and psychological sway of caste in Indian villages.

Pursha (person: head being the Brahmins and feet being Shudras) to whom all the organs/ limbs of the body are of equal value. The analogy breaks down because it does not include people who were outside the caste system, namely Dalits, formerly called *Achutes* (Untouchables). The author contradicts himself (and/or perhaps shows his real thinking) on the notion of equality of different castes by citing examples such as: 'Son of a *low-birth* woman (Sharma 2008: 12); the descended of Satyavati, the low-birth fisherwoman; and Thirukural was a *humble*[19] weaver.' However, there is some support from Srinivas (2002) who says there was some mobility in middle-range castes. But Srinivas also writes that the Untouchables have faced insurmountable difficulties in improving their social position due to the violent resistance of dominant caste Hindus.

On untouchability, Sharma (2008: 24) offers a disingenuous explanation. I quote verbatim: 'In order to avoid life threatening diseases, some castes such as Brahmins, in order to maintain physical purity and remain functional would shun physical contact ... .'

He goes on to argue: 'that such a situation also exists amongst the British in that menial workers seldom interact with the higher echelons ... There are now record levels of homeless people in the UK, who are analogous with the outcastes of Indian society.' I leave the reader to judge the merits or otherwise of such a style of comparison and explanation. But in my view such comparisons are misplaced and conceptually incorrect. Keane (2007: 43) quotes Tambiah to make a clear distinction, for instance, between caste and race:

> Caste embodies purity and impurity; it is an integrated exchange system of
> occupational skills and ritual services; it distributes power in a particular manner;
> it is a way of controlling and restricting marriage ...

The next strand in the thesis is that it is the foreign invaders, especially the British, who coined a new term 'Schedule Castes'[20] to describe the Untouchables. Politically, caste differentiation is also accorded with the British policy of divide and rule to secure the perpetuation of the Raj. Furthermore, their misunderstanding of the caste system was (and is) mainly due to their ignorance (or shallow knowledge) of Sanskrit in which the holy Vedas and other holy scriptures are written.[21] The author posits that deep understanding of Sanskrit is essential to appreciate truly

---

19   Italics are mine to emphasize the inherent inequality in the caste system as is described by Sharma, which he unwittingly approves.

20   This term/description has been retained by successive Indian Governments since Independence in 1947 to deal with policies of reservation (affirmative action) for Untouchables.

21   Sharma (2008: 8) writes: 'As will become clear later in this report, it was as a result of repeated invasions that caste mutated to its current form. A useful measure to preserve Indian heritage, caste adapted as a 'survival mode' response to the need for self-preservation, not the mainstay of Hindu social order, as is currently thought. As for the

the Hindu *varna* system. The present poor conditions of Dalits is mainly due to the past polices of the British Raj, which lasted for nearly three hundred years. Whilst this perspective merits discussion and there is some support from scholars (see Chapter 2), this does not constitute a sound explanation. Distinguished Dalit leaders (Ambedkar, Mangoo Ram, and Kanshi Ram) and scholars (Deliege, 1999; Bayly, 1999) argue that it was high-caste Hindus who excluded the Untouchables from their temples and denied them access to the learning of sacred texts, and that Brahmins have justified and sustained the caste system since its inception. We conclude our comments with a quote from Keane's book (2007: 44) who concludes his survey of literature by emphasizing the uniqueness of the Hindu caste system: 'The mechanism of endogamy in the Hindu context is found in the Vedas and dharma codes. These religious texts ensure the perpetual separation of the castes and provide a spiritual justification for the caste system. There is no caste system outside of Hinduism.'

Concluding Remarks

From the major survey of literature on caste (Bayly, 1999; Mendelsohn and Vicziany 1998; Deliege, 1999) it becomes clear that whichever index of deprivation is considered (income, poverty level, housing, education, employment, ill health and disease, and mortality rate) Untouchables are placed at the bottom of the hierarchy. The majority are slum dwellers or live in mud houses in rural villages and are utterly poor and suffer from a variety of illnesses for which there is little or no medical help. However, due to the reservation of posts in civil service and elsewhere (affirmative action) a tiny minority has entered the middle class strata but they are too few to have wider influence. Marriages are still within caste folds and whenever a couple has defied this tradition punishments have been very severe indeed (see Ghuman, 2003).

Mendelsohn and Vicziany (1998: 263) note that the only significant change after Independence has been the rise of Mayawati and Kanshi Ram other wise 'The overall change we can recognize to be profound has been slow and generational, brought about by the seeping nourishment of the franchise, education, urbanization ... but two factors stand out above all others – *education and the franchise* (my italics).' As we shall see in Chapter 3, confident educated Dalit youth have challenged the hegemony of Jat farmers in a village where they are in majority.

Vedas, the fundamental and authoritative scriptures are concerned; there is no sanction of the caste system.'

He goes on: 'Many Indians believe it to have been a strategy by the East India Company and other foreign parties in India to penetrate the Hindu Indian psyche by interpreting the Vedic scriptures, which underpinned the Hindu mentality and social order. In doing so, they (British) were able to better manipulate the Indian populace thereby facilitating the "divide and rule" policy more effectively.'

Apart from the political success in UP and elsewhere, there are social and cultural forces – similar to the ones made by Ad Dharam in the 1930s – at work to raise the self-esteem, confidence, and pride of Dalits. They want their followers to be proud of their Dalit identity and to this end they are creating and reviving myths, folk tales, and legends of the heroic deeds of their ancestors. Narayan (2006: 20) has spent several years studying this social and cultural phenomenon. He writes:

> In the recent past, however, there is a visible upsurge in the assertion of Dalit identity, which challenges the humiliation that they have faced for centuries. There has emerged a strong urge among these marginalized groups throughout the country to assert their identity and self-respect through their own cultural resources and challenge the hegemony of the upper castes.

This is a sound strategy for the BSP to follow as literature on this topic in social psychology (see Ghuman, 2000) amply testifies to its efficacy.

Chamars who form the majority amongst the Dalits in the Punjab are asserting their self-confidence and corporate identity by challenging the traditional Sikh religious practices in *gurdwaras* by treating their personal gurus/saints on a par with the *Guru Granth Sahib*, the holy book of the Sikhs. The *Hukam Nama* (dictated by the tenth guru Gobind Singh) says that Sikhs should not have any living gurus and treat the holy book as their guru. The argument is that the *Guru Granth Sahib* is composed of hymns and songs of ten Sikh gurus and 24 saints including Sufi Muslims and *bhagat* Ravidas ji. Therefore, the Granth is a repository of wisdom and holiness for its Sikh followers. The second issue is that Chamars think that Ravidas ji should be addressed and treated as a guru and not just a saint and consider him on a par with Sikh gurus in his piety and divinity. Traditional Sikhs refuse to accept this practice and recently this lead to a murder in a *gurdwara* in Austria as noted briefly earlier in the chapter. There was a demonstration of Dalits in London condemning the murder of their revered saint/guru and they demanded their right to worship according to their beliefs. In the Punjab, there were serious riots and the Chief Minister of the Punjab pleaded for peace and held a *bhog* (holy) ceremony at the golden temple in Amritsar in memory of the murdered saint. Manmohan Singh, the Prime Minister of India, who is a Sikh, had to step in to appeal to the good sense of all Punjabis to follow the true spirit of the Sikh religion and show respect and tolerance to all sects of Sikhism.

It is within this context that we have to view the position of Dalit communities in the UK. They, like any other immigrant community, have brought their cultural baggage, life styles, aspirations, and indeed worldviews with them. They bring with them memories of their long-standing suffering because of social exclusion and gross discrimination which persisted over two millennia. Many have personal experiences of caste oppression, discrimination, and social stigma to deal with. In the ensuing chapters, we relate their stories and their attempts to adjust to life in the UK and to fight for fair play and justice from people of Indian origins and from the members of the host society.

Chapter 3

A Case Study of Untouchables in a Punjabi Village: Class a New Avatar of Caste

This chapter reports the findings of a case study which was carried out to investigate to what extent the lives of Dalits have changed over half a century. The focus of the paper is on Dalit women as they have been exploited by their men and high-caste people. In addition, the detailed fieldwork should illustrate in a vivid way the lived experience of Dalits, and inter-caste relationships in one village. The writer has a great deal of personal experience of the village under study and will weave it into the narrative, which is chiefly based on interviews and textual sources. From her authoritative historical survey of caste in India from eighteenth century to the contemporary scene Bayly (1999: 382) concludes:

> It may even be that one day the principles and usages of jati and varna will lose much or all of their meaning for Indians living both within and beyond the subcontinent. Nevertheless, if one is to do justice to its complex history, and its contemporary culture and politics, caste must be neither disregarded nor downplayed – its power has simply been too compelling and enduring.

Likewise, there are other researchers who endorse the significance of caste in the Indian way of life. According to Chakravarti (2003), the ideology of caste still governs the lives of Hindu communities as well as that of Muslim, Christian, and Sikh communities who have kept alive their caste identities. Quigley (1994) argues that in the last decade alone scores of ethnographies from all over South Asia have come to the conclusion that caste continues to be a bedrock of the social organization of hundreds of millions of people.

Notwithstanding the validity of the above generalizations which apply to millions of people with enormous religious and cultural diversity, the researcher was interested in finding out how far these observations apply to a village community in the Punjab. To place the lives of those in the community in context, the writer briefly compares the economic, social, and religious conditions of Dalits in the 1950s (a few years after Indian Independence – August 1947) with their present-day situation and achievements. I start with a lengthy quote from an elderly grandmother whom I have known for over 50 years:

> Oh yes, there has been a sea change since the days of your parents and when you left for England. We were not allowed to go near the water pump. We used to cup our hands to drink water. The S … granny thought we would pollute the

water supply and shooed us out. She always asked the elderly Brahmin woman to purify the pump by reciting mantras – mumbo jumbo [laughs]. Now, her grandchildren, who live abroad, have handed over the looking after the house to us. We use their *chula* (kitchen) and other facilities. The irony of the situation is that when they visit the village they say we enjoy chappatis and vegetables made by my granddaughter ... The changes are mind blowing. We are invited by Jats (farming caste) to their weddings and religious ceremonies and they attend ours. It is really fantastic. (82-year-old grandmother – translated from Punjabi, Oct. 2006)

The narrative of this chapter is based on intensive semi-structured interviews with 16 people (four from each category of gender and two castes[1]) and protracted observations for several weeks in November 2006. Topics covered in the interviews include: jobs, agricultural labour, inter-caste relationship, social interaction, religious orientation, segregation in *gurdwaras* and village cemetery, reservation issues, schooling and education. An informal group discussion between Dalits and farmers (Jat Sikh) was held to air their views on the topics used in the interviews. Extensive field-notes were made on Dalit families and their life style and Dalit *gurdwaras* to make comparison with the situation in the 1950s. The writer has kept a journal of his observations on the salient changes in the village demography and social and political organization since he left the Punjab in 1959 (see Ghuman, 1975). Lengthy extracts from interviews are used to illuminate issues under discussion.

Broader Jat-Dalit Relationships in North India

The nature of caste relationships in north India, especially in the Punjab, is quite different to that found in the rest of India.[2] In this region land-owning Jats form the dominant caste and have employed Chamars and Valmikis as agricultural labourers. Their economic and social position until the late 1940s was little better than the degrading treatment of serfs in feudal Russia in that most of them were tied to a particular household by the *jajmani*[3] social system. Although since Independence in August 1947 several laws have been passed guaranteeing equal rights and making untouchability a criminal offence, the economic and social position of

---

1   Jats, whose main occupation is farming, and Dalits, who are composed of Chamar (leather workers) and Valmikis, Churas, and Bhangis, whose traditional occupation was/is cleaning farming sheds, lavatories, and roads.

2   In other parts of India Brahmins and Kshatriya – also called twice born – are mainly the two dominant castes.

3   Dumont (2004: 98) gives a comprehensive explanation of this social arrangement. But briefly landowning castes pay the servicing castes in kind with grain or other products. The 'redistribution often takes place on the threshing floor ... The relationships are hereditary and personal and tinged with patronage' (Seymour-Smith, 1986).

Dalits has not changed significantly. There are a few ethnographic studies (Bhatia, 2006; Jodhka, 2004; Ram, 2004a, b) which highlight the disadvantaged position of Dalits in a caste hierarchy. Bhatia carried out his study in Chakwada village (Jaipur, Rajasthan) to analyse the factors underlying the Dalit rebellion against untouchability. Dalits of the village wanted to exercise their civic rights to bathe in the village reservoir, had been denied them by the dominant Jat caste since its inception. Jats mobilized their community from several villages and threatened to use physical force to keep the Dalits from bathing there. According to Bhatia, this was a clear case of re-affirmation of Jat caste identity, and their explicit aim was to impose their traditional belief of caste hierarchy on Dalits. They achieved their goal by virtue of their economic hegemony, numerical strength, and political power. He concludes: 'Caste-based hierarchy and power are still at the heart of the traditional social order and determine to large extent, the kinds of lives that people live. Further, the police and the state machinery have failed the constitutional rights of Dalits, and often end up aligning with forces that suppress them' (Bhatia, 2006: 57). He asserts that this is not an isolated case of one village but that it is widespread throughout India. In a wide-ranging review paper Jodhka (2004: 181) describes the positions of Dalits in Punjabi villages succinctly: 'Caste continues to be an important marker of social, economic and political life in contemporary Punjab. Caste based segregation is easily evident in the social life in rural Punjab.'

Local Context

Kiranhari (fictitious name) village is situated some two miles away from a city *Zeda* which is a district headquarters in the Punjab. The city is prosperous and serves as a market town. It has several high schools, a degree-awarding college, banks, and several government offices, including an office of a Deputy Commissioner – an IAS officer who wields a great deal of authority and is held in very high esteem due to his personal integrity. The present holder of this post happens to be a Dalit, as is the senior police superintendent. Both these executive posts are important to keep in mind in relation to the subject matter as will become clear.[4]

Before the partition of India in 1947, the majority of the population of the village consisted of Muslims who were the sole landowners. This is attested by the fact that there were three mosques (which thrive but in a neglected state) to cater for the religious needs of the villagers. During Partition Muslims from the Indian Punjab (called East Punjab) fled to Pakistan and Sikhs and Hindus from the Pakistani West Punjab likewise came to India. The village population in the 1950s was composed of Sikh farmers, service castes (sometimes referred to as Shudras and consisting of *jhir* (water carriers), *tarkhans* (carpenters), *lohars* (blacksmiths),

---

4   Bob (2007: 190) writes: 'Dalit activists argue that police forces, composed of higher caste Hindus, have failed to prevent atrocities against them and, in many cases, have condoned or participated in such violence.'

and *jhulahas* (weavers), and Dalits, also referred to as Harijans, Untouchables, and
Scheduled Castes.[5]

The economic and social situation of Dalits in the Punjabi villages in the 1950s
and 1960s has been soundly discussed by Juergensmeyer (1982) in his seminal
book. His conclusions are based on in-depth fieldwork in three Punjabi villages,
interviews with dozens of eminent Dalits (including Mangoo Ram, the founder of
the Ad Dharam movement[6] in the Punjab), and an extensive survey and appraisal
of literature in the field. He concludes:

> As we observed earlier, village Untouchables in the Punjab are virtually
> synonymous with the economic class of landless labourers. As such, they have
> seldom had opportunities for economic development ... In the 1960s it seemed
> that the 'Green revolution' would enable the Punjab to give the lie to Dandekar's
> pessimisms ... but in more recent years the gap between the upper castes and
> landless labourers has become more severe than ever before, and the long-range
> forecast does not seem more hopeful (Juergensmeyer, 1982: 231).

In Kiranhari village the economic position of Dalits was similar to the one
described by Juergensmeyer. It is also relevant to note here the way Beteille (as
quoted by Deliege 1999: 8) described the dire situation of Untouchables in a south
Indian village in the 1960s: 'Socio-economic dependence, material poverty, social
deprivation and lack of political power combine with ritual pollution to make
Untouchables a social category clearly set apart from the rest of society.' Although
the position of Dalits in the village under study was not as dire as in the village
Beteille studied, its findings resonate with the plight of Dalits in our village. It
may be instructive to cite here the conclusion reached by Dumont (2004: 106) in
his classic book *Homo Hierarchicus* on the position of the dominant caste (like
Jat Sikh in our research), vis-à-vis Dalits in Indian villages: 'All other castes are
dependent. Roughly speaking, their members (that is, Scheduled castes) obtain
direct or indirect access to the means of subsistence through personal relationships
with the members of the dominant caste, in virtue of the functions which they are
fit to perform and which the dominant caste requires.'

My observations (Ghuman, 1975) on the village community broadly confirm the
above generalization, except that the policy of reservation[7] for Dalits in education
and employment was beginning to produce a few middle-class professionals who
were forcefully articulating the poor economic conditions of their community.

---

5   The Constitution of India defines them as Scheduled Castes but they prefer to call
themselves Dalits – the oppressed ones. Gandhi called them Harijans – children of god. But
Dalits resent this label and consider it condescending (see Keane, 2007: 4–14).

6   See Chapter 2.

7   The Constitution of India prescribes reservation (affirmative action) of 25 per cent
(raised to 50) places in educational establishments and government jobs.

The current total population of the village is not available but the total number of households is approximately 500 (ascertained from a *lamberdar* – one of the headmen in the village). Eighty-eight per cent of the households belong to Dalit communities which include Chamars, also called Ad Dharmis and Valmikis. There are eight households (just fewer than two per cent) belonging to backward *jatis* known as *jhirs* (water carriers) and *tarkhnas* (carpenters). Five households (ten per cent) are composed of Jat Sikhs, farmers who own all the land in the village. There was a single Brahmin family who left some thirty years ago and settled in a city. There are three *gurdwaras* in the village: two of them are run by the Ad Dharmi community and the third is managed and attended mainly by the farmer community. Although, *gurdwaras* are meant to be shared by all, the Hindu caste divisions have crept into Sikhism in an attenuated form. There is one Valmiki temple in an embryonic form for the 30 Valmiki families. Also, there are three tombstones which are venerated by a few Chamar families. Such a mode of worship may be classified as ancestral worship (*Babane dhe puja* in Punjabi). There are two cemeteries in the village, one for the farming community and the other for Dalits.[8] Although there are no rigid restrictions on where funerals/cremations take place, caste divisions are usually observed.

Although the author has lived in the UK since 1959, he has been a regular visitor and stayed for his vacations in his ancestral village. There have been major demographic and social changes in the village since the 1950s. Two important ones which concern us here relate to the emigration of Jat families to Australia, Europe, the US, and Canada, and the large increase of Dalit families and their improved financial position. A number of Dalit men have gone to Dubai and other Arab emirates to work and save money to improve their financial position in the village. Many Dalit men are working in a near by sugar mill and others have sought jobs in government sponsored projects and organizations. Virtually none of them works on the farms now, which is in sharp contrast to the 1950s when virtually all of them worked as agricultural labourers. This has enhanced their political and social standing in the village.

The Dalit population has increased dramatically because of their traditional attitude to family planning: four to five children were considered quite normal for a family in the 1950s and 1960s. The thinking behind this was that children are earning members of the family as domestic and farm labourers. Furthermore, the belief was that their children would support them in their old age as there was no provision for pensions or any other welfare scheme. The farmers on the other hand became conscious of the cost of rearing and educating children and started using birth control methods to keep the family to two or three children. Another major factor which has reduced their number is emigration. Attracted by the high standard of living and good educational and economic opportunities abroad, farmers' progeny have emigrated in large numbers to the UK, North America, Australia, and Europe.

---

8   Some Dalits bury their dead whereas the farming community invariably cremate.

Thus the emigration of young farmers and the rise of the Dalit population have dramatically altered the power structure and inter-caste relationship in the village. High-school and college-educated Dalit young men and women are quite radical (even militant) and reject the old hegemony of farming families in all manner of things. A Dalit bank clerk interviewed for this research observed:

> We totally reject the dominance of farming people over us. Our forefathers were subjected to a variety of humiliations. It upsets me terribly to think of those times. Our community was mercilessly exploited. There were rapes of our women and our whole families worked for them for pittance. They took advantage of our economic dependence and lack of education and enriched themselves. Now we are seeking government jobs and are working in nearby city and don't care for the farm work.

Dalits' Education in the Village

Education is considered to be a means of social mobility and is highly desired by minority groups all over the world. There is a deep-seated belief in the Punjab that education imparts knowledge and wisdom which is priceless. A popular saying is: 'A thief can steal your jewellery and rob you of your possessions but cannot deprive you of your knowledge.' Dr Ambedkar, the founding father of the modern Dalit movement, urged his followers to '*educate, unite, and agitate*'. As described in Chapter 2, he was an exceptionally highly educated Dalit having gained higher degrees from England and the US and was the chief architect of the Indian Constitution.

The village under study had a primary school in the 1950s staffed by a single teacher. There were approximately 100 children and the school was housed in two rooms with a veranda, and the teacher had to organize his teaching around this space with the help of school monitors. There was no furniture to speak of in the school. Children sat on mats and the teacher had a chair, a desk, and an easel on which to place a blackboard. Although the school was open to boys and girls of all castes, very few girls were allowed to attend by their parents and very rarely Dalit boys were spared by their parents from labouring work. The Dalit parents' argument was: 'we need the agricultural wages of our boys to feed our families and the girls to help with household chores.' Schooling was very traditional and the main focus was to teach children the 3Rs. Discipline was strict and maintained by free use of corporal punishment which was supported by most parents.

There has been a sea-change in the village schooling. The school has been upgraded to a middle school (up to the age of 15) and there are five teachers and several new classrooms with desks and chairs for the students. There are reading and maths books for the children who are encouraged to borrow books and read at home. Although teaching methods are still traditional, teachers use charts and simple aids to make their lessons interesting. The school curriculum has broadened to include the teaching of science, geography, and history.

However, the school intake is now chiefly from Dalit families and there are only a handful of children belonging to higher castes. The latter send their children to private fee-paying schools in the nearby city – as do the more affluent Dalit families. Therefore segregation of children along caste lines continues right from the primary school.

It is not only the caste snobbery which has lead to this situation but the poor quality of teaching and education in village schools. Teachers employed in village schools are fully qualified and well paid but many of them are often absent (frequently with the collusion of head teachers) and are engaged in running their own private businesses. I quote from a report undertaken by an independent body and reported in a Panjabi newspaper: 'In one district (Muktsar) 26 teachers were absent, 61 were late and five Principals were on an unauthorised leave (*Jag Banni*: 28 November, 2006: 4).

Teachers during the school hours do not take their professional responsibility seriously. A parent explained:

> Many teachers are women teachers in primary schools. It is a second salary for them – and it is very good now. They are interested in their pay and do not care for the education of children. They talk all day and knit things for their families and generally idle away their time at school. Men are little more serious but they also gossip away their time ... Think of running their private business and so on ...

Nobel Laureate, Amartya Sen (2005: 216) describes a similar situation in West Bengal schools:

> A major difficulty lies in the weak institutional structure of primary schools in much of India, which are often inefficiently run ... A significant proportion of teachers were absent from schools on the days which we visited them unannounced. Teachers absenteeism was very much greater in schools where the bulk of the pupils come from Scheduled Caste or Scheduled Tribe (Dalit) families; indeed 75 per cent of these schools in our list had serious problem of teacher absenteeism ... very large proportion of children rely on private tuition ... Indeed, of the pupils in Classes 3 and 4 we could test, the vast majority of those who did not get private tuition could not even sign their names.

In sum, the village school has improved compared to the 1950s but the quality of education delivered to their charges is still poor compared with private fee-paying schools due to large class sizes (over 50), meagre resources, and poorly motivated teachers. This is a typical picture of village schools in the Punjab, which has negative consequences for the further and university education of Dalit children. The professional and middle-class Dalits tend to opt out of the state system and thereby weaken the accountability of teachers to the parents. The middle-class parents as elsewhere are articulate and aware of their rights and can hold teachers, who enjoy good pay, pension and holidays, to account.

Thus the state school system is reinforcing the caste and class divisions rather than integrating the different elements of society. In a group discussion with Dalit activists in Birmingham I was told that:

> Education does not change anything in India as Public (state) schools which are under-resourced and staffed with poor teachers are attended by Dalits. Teachers do not want to educate these kids, and even if they do, it is an uphill task – two teachers to a class of say hundred children. Education system reinforces the social system rather than changing it. We need societal change rather than tinkering with small issues and problems …

These remarks reveal the cynical attitudes of many Dalits who are frustrated by the pace of change and the way in which their communities always get a raw deal because of the way in which social inequality is structured and perpetuated in Punjabi society.

This background introduction should help the reader to appreciate the keen interest and enthusiasm shown by Dalits towards the education of their progeny in the UK and elsewhere in the West.

Dalit Women in the Village

The patriarchal structure of families is still a norm for the vast majority of Indians. Women's positions and roles are still considered to be different, and inferior, to those of men, although this is changing especially amongst the middle classes in the urban areas. In general, Dalit women are perceived to be at the bottom of the social hierarchy of Indian society. Ruth Manoroma, a Dalit activist, refers to Dalit women as 'the thrice discriminated … She is a Dalit among Dalits (Quoted in Hardtmann, 2003: 195) and rhetorically argues: 'Why are only Dalit women paraded naked? Why does the *devdasi*[9] and bonded labour tradition exist among Dalits only?' (*The Tribune*, 28 February, 2007). Chakarvati (2003, 143) confirms the three-fold oppression faced by Dalit women viz., of caste, class, and patriarchal structure of family.

A Dalit woman's testimony speaks eloquently of their desperate plight:

> When I got married my husband told me to clean lavatories which involved cleaning human faeces all morning by my bare hands. After a few days, I refused to carry on because it was making me ill … I could not bear the foul stench and appalling conditions of lavatories. My husband called my father and told him that I am refusing to obey him … My father sent my brother who told me that I have to obey my husband

---

9   Rough rendering of this term would be a temple prostitute.

because this is our custom. Now I have to do it. Everyday I feel sick and do not want
to eat anything in the morning (http://www.idsn.org/movie/dalit.htm).

In the 1950s most of the high-caste people would use the fields for calls of nature as
is the custom in most Punjabi villages. However, there were four families including
two retired public school teachers, who paid cash to Valmiki women to clean their
lavatories. Valmiki women did clean the farm sheds of farming families for which they
were paid in kind, such as with half a ton of wheat and maize, *shukkhar* (raw sugar)
annually, and fodder for their cattle. Dalit women in the village also did odd jobs for
farmers' families where their husbands worked as labourers. These included: cleaning
houses and courtyards, grinding and sifting corn, winnowing, fetching and carrying
things, and other small errands. They were not allowed in kitchens and whenever they
were given cooked food it was always in 'special' utensils which were kept separately
specifically for them.

Some men from the farming families took Dalit women as free and handy sexual
partners and thought it was their right to do so (see Mendelsohn and Vicziany, 1998). I
was shocked to hear a quip from a farmer, made in 1957, which is etched in my memory:

> Any Dalit woman who comes to collect fodder and grass for their cattle or for firewood
> etc. in our fields is a fair game … They dare not make a fuss because we would ban
> them from our fields and they cannot afford to do that …

This is so remote from today's situation that it feels like the village has been catapulted
into modernity from the dark ages. When I told a farmer's son of this degrading
treatment of Dalit women in the 1950s he was shocked and said:

> *Toba, toba* (thousand apologies and regrets), that sort of thing cannot happen now.
> They will be banged up in jail for ever. Both the DC and the senior superintendent of
> the Police are Dalits … By the way, there is a mandatory jail sentence for insulting
> Dalits – calling them by old rude names such as Chamars and Churas. For this offence
> there is no bail either … (Translated from Punjabi, Nov. 2006)

However, evidence from other Indian states suggests that sexual exploitation of Dalit
women continues, if somewhat at a reduced frequency (Pawde, 1995). A comment by
a Swiss scholar is most interesting: 'A schedule caste woman lacks morality just by
being born into this category, and again, this should be "proved" or shown to her and
to the world. This may be done either by rape, by "parading her naked" or by exposing
her sexual and private life (in the case of Mayawati) or the sexual aggressions against
her (Phulan Devi)'[10] (Hardtmann, 2003: 190–1).

---

10   Phulan Devi was gang raped by high-caste people and when she complained to the
police she was raped by them. She joined an outlaw gang (*dacoits*) and took revenge on the
people who raped her and the oppressed people. She shot them all. She was imprisoned but
later pardoned and became an MP. She has become a legend for Dalit women.

Inter-caste Marriages

The bedrock of the caste system, and its reproduction, is in the ingrained tradition of endogamous marriages. Marriages used to be arranged (and most of them still are) on caste/*varna* considerations with the help of close relatives. Nowadays, however, newspapers and the internet have become favourite media for matchmaking, especially for the rising middle-class families. An example from a daily English newspaper carries hundreds of advertisements such as:

> Match for Sarsawat Brahmin (mohyal) PH.D., 75 born, 5–3/12, lecturer in …

These appear under caste headings: Saini, Vaish Jain, Hindu Khatri, Arora, Sikh Jat, Schedule Caste, and so on. Punjabi and Hindi newspapers carry such advertisements usually on Sunday. This practice continues amongst Indians settled in the UK and North America.

Inter-caste marriages are very rare indeed and when a brave soul ventures he/she has to pay a heavy price, resulting in social isolation and emotional turmoil. A farmer told me this story:

> A bloke from a Jhir family ran away with a Valmiki girl and the couple is in hiding as they have been disowned by their families. The village *Panchyat* (council) is supporting the families and have condemned the run away couple … So it is very rarely that such unions are approved. This is even more so with the Jat and Chamar families.

Women carry the *izzat* (honour) of the family as daughters, wives to be and later as mothers. Although even now many Dalit women carry out traditional work on the farm, they do so with dignity and without fear of sexual harassment and insults. Some of them now work as domestics and cook food etc. in farmers' households. A comment of a Jat woman is illuminating:

> We have no choice … There is nobody to help us. Our kids are abroad or working away and we cannot manage … Although I draw a line. I say only Chamars but not Churas … [this was said in a hushed voice – the latter are still associated with cleaning lavatories and eating carrion] … I say they are spoiled now by the successive governments … Jobs are reserved as are places in universities for them. They are entitled now to state pensions, and 15,000 rupees grant on their daughter's weddings. So I say what about the poor Jat farmers and their children? (Eighty-year-old housewife)

Her tone and expressions suggested a grudging acceptance of middle-class Chamar families and those considered to be clean to work in the kitchen.

Views on Affirmative Action/ Reservation

A recent law (*Guardian*, 17 May, 2006) passed by the Central Government of India stipulates that nearly 50 per cent of places in universities and higher institutes of teaching should be reserved for Scheduled Castes, Scheduled Tribes, and Other Backward Classes.[11] This has created a great deal of friction between the Dalits and farmer communities in the village and nationally. This became quite apparent in my interviews with both groups. A Dalit (retired Captain) opined:

> I see ... May be reservation should be based on financial situation of the family. I am better off than many Jat farmers but my grandchildren will get this advantage ...

But when I talked to farmers they opined that Dalits are not revealing their true feelings on the subject. A 72-year-old farmer amplified his resentment:

> Now listen! Why should a son of a DC (Deputy Commissioner), who gets 60 per cent marks, be given preference over a poor Jat's son who scores the same percentage? After all the former had all the advantages and privileges and the latter probably attended a village school with poor facilities. A case has been cited where a candidate obtained 80 per cent marks and was denied admission ... Is this fair? Even the High Court has referred this matter of a 'creamy layer' and reservation to the Central Government for consideration. The high court judges deemed it unfair ... but the Central Government will get around it somehow because they rely on the Dalit 'vote bank.'

The farmer is not entirely correct on the exclusion of a creamy layer[12] from the reservation of government posts at provincial and federal (central) levels. The landmark judgement of the Indian Supreme Court in 1993 ruled that (Verma, N., 2005: 382): 'Within four months of the date of judgement the Government of India shall specify the bases, applying the relevant and requisite socio-economic criteria to exclude socially advanced persons/sections ("creamy layer") from the "Other Backward Classes."[13] Under the Chairmanship of Prasad the Committee on 'creamy layer' worked out the detailed criteria for exclusion from reservation

---

11   Scheduled Castes refers to that category of citizens previously known as 'Untouchables', 'Harijans', and now, Dalits. Scheduled Tribes are known by their tribal culture and geographical location. Other Backward Classes is a wide-ranging term denoting those citizens who are low in the social hierarchy, but do not belong to a Scheduled Caste (Keane, 2007: 127). Other Backward Classes include, for example, *lohar* (blacksmiths), *tarkhans* (carpenters), and *jhirs* (water carriers).

12   This only applies to former Untouchables (schedule castes) see the following note.

13   Other Backward Classes were recommended 27 per cent of government jobs; this does not include the former Untouchables who already had 22 per cent of the total posts.

(Verma, R., 2005: 144). For instance, it excludes all Class 1 and 11 officers and military personnel holding the rank of colonel (or higher) and families whose yearly income is one lakh or over (1,400 pounds sterling). Many state governments had already developed their own criteria for exclusion but these were largely in accord with the recommendation of the Prasad Committee.[14]

However, the debate is still raging over 'creamy layer' reservation. The argument is that even the privileged Scheduled Castes (former Untouchables) are enjoying reservation in education, employment, and promotion whilst the poor people of higher castes, and even poor Dalits, are not obtaining their fare share. A 40-year-old farmer's son explained:

> I know of a village Dalit girl who obtained her MA and was advised by her well-off relatives to try for the IAS (Indian Administrative Services – considered to be the most prestigious) examination. Her father sent her to a coaching academy as is the custom amongst aspiring candidates. Within a couple of weeks she dropped out as she could not make any sense of what was going on. It was well above her head ... she was a village Dalit girl who was amongst the sons and daughters of privileged elite families – including Dalits ... So we say that affirmative action and reservation should be based on financial position of a family rather than on caste. But they do not care ... it is the 'vote bank' the Congress is after.

In our view, most Dalits support reservation not only in government employment but also in the private sector on the grounds that two millennia of injustices and inhumanity cannot be addressed within 60 years or so. Furthermore the argument runs that the vast majority of Dalits are amongst the poorest in Indian society anyway. In a recent speech the Indian Prime Minister Manmohan Singh (*Guardian*, 28 December 2006) described the situation of Dalits in India as the same as positions of blacks in South Africa prior to the dismantling of the apartheid structure: 'Dalits have faced a unique discrimination in our society that is fundamentally different from the problems of minority groups in general. The only parallel to the practice of untouchability was apartheid.'

Segregation Continues

I was most surprised to learn that there are still separate/segregated cemeteries for Daltis when I talked to a farmer:

> I say to the village folks: 'Look *gurdwaras* and cemeteries should belong – and indeed be shared – by all the village community, but there are traditionalist farmers who do not like such a way of thinking. So what can we do? However,

---

14   Since the passing of the Supreme Court ruling on OBCs there have been several other judgements since 1993 that have modified some aspects of its landmark judgement. For details, see Chapter 3 of Keane's book (2007).

there are no rigid rules ... the other day a Dalit family used our graveyard for a funeral and it was OK. Dalits are backed by high officers of the district now so these backward thinking people dare not make a fuss ... Alas, such traditions die hard as you know Guru Nanak (the founder of Sikh religion) preached and practised equality and was dead against caste. But the institution of Hindu priesthood (literate and influential) was too powerful to see the caste system disappear ... Even now many Sikh families are lead by Brahmin priests. Brahmins are full of guile and mislead people into *believing all sorts of gods and rituals which could bring them prosperity, prestige and good health* ... (see also Srinivas, 2002: 237).

Likewise a retired Dalit Sikh army officer (full beard and turban) ruminated:

In the Army there are no caste distinctions. We are there to fight for our country and you are promoted and judged on your merit. The village norms and politics are very different. We have three *gurdwaras* along the caste lines and also there are two cemeteries ... Now this is against the tenets of Sikh religion and 'common humanity' ... I tried to stay as long as I could in the Army (Some 40 years) as I enjoyed its 'ethos'.

A Valmiki woman had this to say on her own community's place of worship

We have a small room for our services as there are not that many families who attend regularly. We intend to extend our place but there are no funds available for our project. Chamars have built *gurdwaras* with the help of the Jat community. (Do you go to there?) No, we worship Bhagvan Valmiki and keep *Ramayana* in our room whereas Chamars have the Sikh *Guru Granth Sahib* ... We are different from them.

In some districts of the Punjab (Amritsar and Gurdaspur) most Valmikis[15] have converted to Sikhism and they attend mainstream Sikh *gurdwaras* and are very proud of their contribution to Sikh religion. But the majority Jat communities do not accept them on equal terms. It is clear that Sikhs have not purged their religion of caste distinctions, and that even amongst the Untouchables there is caste awareness/consciousness. According to my interviewees, most Chamars in the village look down upon the Valmikis because they are on the lower rung of the Untouchable caste ladder. They do not mix socially with them and do not invite them to their weddings and religious ceremonies. A Chamar told me:

---

15   Many Valmikis in Jalander City converted to Christianity to escape discrimination and daily humiliation but regrettably the stigma of being an Untouchable never vanished (Juergensmeyer, 1982).

These people [Valmikis] used to clean toilets and animal sheds and now are mainly sweepers ... They do the dirtiest jobs. We on the other hand worked on the farms and now have our businesses or work in factories.

Likewise, there is caste snobbery amongst the artisan caste (service caste) which is again based on a self-perceived and socially approved hierarchy. For instance a goldsmith considers himself socially higher than a blacksmith and he in turn thinks himself higher than a weaver.

Inter-caste Relationships

Social interaction in the 1950s was governed entirely by caste considerations. Farmers' invitations on the birth of sons (not baby daughters!), weddings, and thanks-giving religious ceremonies invariably excluded the village Dalits. Those farm-hands who were allowed at the parties ate separately (two glass system) and after the high castes had eaten were often given the leftovers. Caste boundaries were strictly observed.

By today the situation has changed dramatically. An elderly Dalit woman gave a detailed account:

> There is a sea-change now in social mixing and interacting. When my grand daughter was married we invited selected Jat families. They all came and joined in performing *Shaggan* (engagement) ceremonies and then they ate with us. We are invited to their weddings and we are happy to attend and are treated with respect ... Gone are the days when we have to stay out of their houses and were the last to receive leftover food. We had to bring our own plates as we were supposed to defile/pollute their plates ... Things have changed for the better.

A farmer gave a following account of the social interaction:

> Look, things have changed radically in our village (this is not the case with every village by the way – things are still very traditional). We Jats invite selected Dalit families to our special social and religious 'occasions' as they invite us to theirs. These families have moved up the social ladder. They are business people or former government and retired military officers. They are all educated and send their children to private schools. Their houses are clean and they no longer indulge in rampant smoking and so on. A number of them have embraced our religion i.e. Sikhism and are more *pucka* than many of the Jats. Now our Guru Nanak preached equality and fellowship of all ... .[I interposed and asked why were they rejected in the past]. Well, the thing is that then they ate carrion, smoked, and were dirty and unhygienic. So it was their life style rather than caste which we objected to as I told you before. Our religion is against caste practices.

Caste and Class

The notion of class kept on cropping up in my interviews with Dalits and Jat interviewees in a variety of ways. The gist of their conversations appeared to be that when families do well and have a good standard of living, own *pucka* houses and their children go to private schools, then it is quite natural for people of various castes to mix. Several interviewees mentioned that the 'equality' status of Dalits is backed by law and that there are Dalit senior officers who will see that they do not suffer any type of abuse. The village *Panchayat* (Council) is now dominated by Dalit officers as Jats are in a minority and this has boosted Dalits' confidence and morale.

A young Dalit told me:

> We take the lead in village affairs now as the Jats are elderly and are in minority. Most of the young Jats have emigrated to other countries so we young Dalits are in charge … Jats have helped us to build *gurdwaras*; but some of us would like Guru Ravidas *bhavans*.[16]

A young Jat (one of the very few remaining in the village) expressed his fears:

> The majority are Dalits in the village and they will take over our homes and land eventually, I fear … A plot of land is given free to Dalits who want to build a house. Now there is no common land left and it will come out of Jats' land. The government will pay us the minimum rates and so it goes on. We are losing out.

Table 3.1 summarizes the socio-economic changes since the 1950s.

It is appropriate here to relate the findings of our study with a similar study carried out by Selvam (2000) in a village called Vagikulam in the Madurai region of south Indian. The researcher compares the socio-economic position of Untouchables in 1950s and in 1990. He found remarkable improvement in the building material of the houses: by and large *pucka* houses have replaced mud built houses in the village. However, unlike our village, the high-caste houses are segregated from those of the Dalits. Payment in kind to agricultural labourers has ceased and now they are paid an hourly wage. He concludes (Selvam 2000: 41) that 'the process of change that sociologist describe, the mobility, is meagre among the Untouchables who fall outside the four tiered caste system, and occupy the bottom of the social hierarchy … .' Our findings resonate with this conclusion. Selvam finds hardly any inter-caste relations in the marital and familial domains in the lives of the people under study. For example, he notes that members of the

----

16 Although Guru Ravidas ji's hymns are included in the *Adi Granth* (holy book of Sikhs) he is only referred to as a *Bhagat* (saint) and is not considered of the same holy status as the Sikh gurus. But this is likely to change (see Chapter 7).

Table 3.1   Comparison of socio-economic status and religious orientations of Dalits

1950s[a] primary school in the village – poor attendance of Dalit children	2006 middle (age 15) school in the village – good attendance of Dalit children
They were completely dependent on farm work; often whole families were tied to a farmer. No welfare payment of any kind.	They work in state-sponsored projects or nearby city mills; farm workers are Dalits from Bihar and UP. There is a pension for the seniors and grants are available for girls' weddings.
They lived in mud huts with their own wells for water. Lived in segregated areas of the village called *Chamarli*.	They live in *pucka* houses with electricity and tap water or with their own hand pumps. No segregation now.
Religious orientation: ancestral worship and '*guga pir puja*' (snake worship) but no temples.	There are two *gurdwaras*, a Valmiki *Bhavan* but some form of ancestral worship still continues.
Ritual untouchability and segregation was the norm. Marriages were endogamous.	Ritual untouchability has completely disappeared but there is *de facto* segregation in *gurdwaras* and cemeteries. Marriages are still endogamous.
Dalit women were grossly exploited and oppressed by Jat farmers and their own men.	Gross exploitation (especially sexual) has ceased and women are aware of their rights, and these are being enforced by local senior Dalit government officials.
There was no Dalit middle class as such.	Rising Dalit middle class have had an impact on village affairs.
Although Dalits were in majority they accepted the hegemony of Jat Sikh farmers in all manner of village affairs.	Dalits are in vast majority and run the village affairs through the elected *Panchayat* – village council.

[a] Details of village school and children's education are given in Appendix A.

higher castes do not inter-dine or exchange utensils with the Dalits.[17] This type of ritual untouchability has disappeared from Kiranhari, as discussed.

---

17   I have exchanged e-mails (July 2007) with Prof. Selvam on the situation of the Dalits of the village he studied in 1999. He tells me that 'no longer are there separate tea/coffee glasses for Dalits who sit in one corner of the shops. This was not the case ten years ago ... However, they do not come and draw water from the well belonging to high caste Hindus.' He sent me a cutting from the *Hindu* newspaper (14 April 2007) which carried out a survey on Untouchables in villages in the Madurai district. The article offers evidence of extensive discrimination based on the untouchability of Dalits. Here is the concluding line: 'As many as 17 Dalit Panchayat presidents in Madurai admit that caste-based discrimination, including "tow-tumbler" system, still exists in their villages ... Doctors and para-medical staff refused to touch Dalit patients.'

He notes that the physical abuse of Dalits in the studied village continues which is completely in contrast to the treatment of Dalits in our research. This is partly due to the fact – noted in the introduction to this chapter – that senior civil and police officers are Dalits and would take action should any incidence of physical or verbal abuse be reported. In sum, we find only a few similarities, but many differences with Selvam's research findings. This may point up the chief difference between north and south India on the treatment of Dalits, which was described earlier in this chapter. A large-scale study by Jodhka (2004) is of great interest here as he carried out an extensive study of 24 Punjabi villages on contemporary issues on 'caste and structure of social relations'. The researcher says that the position of Punjabi Dalits in villages is/was radically different from that of villages in the South in that untouchability was never as brutal, mainly owing to the mediating message of equality found in Sikhism and Islam. He found that Dalits are building their own religious places of worship (*gurdwaras* and *mandirs*) and community centres to renew their spiritual and cultural resources (also see Ram, 2004a, b). Furthermore according to his findings, Dalits have developed self-confidence and pride by disassociating themselves from their traditional work of tanning leather and the like, and have liberated themselves from bonded agricultural work. They have opened small businesses and trained themselves as barbers, mechanics, and blacksmiths. Many of them are now working in nearby mills and government sponsored projects. In sum Jodhka says (2004: 189): 'The processes of dissociation, distancing and autonomy … show that the Dalits of Punjab are breaking out of the systemic aspects of caste … However, once freed from old structures, they also make claims over the common resources of the village and begin to demand equal rights vis-à-vis other caste communities.' Our findings accord with the main conclusions of his research. It is interesting to note here that in-depth case studies can often reveal as much as large-scale studies and save effort and resources. However, both are important to unravel the intricacies of the social processes under investigation and should be used according to the remit of the inquiry.

Conclusions

Dalit families are no longer dependent on Jat Sikh families to provide them farm work and from this flows many things. Dalit women do not go the fields, as they did in the 1950s, to gather wood and fodder for their domestic animals. Dalit men have developed self-confidence and belief in their own abilities to undertake major responsibilities in village affairs. Dalits are in majority and in the nearby city Dalits occupy senior civil and police jobs. Young Jat Sikhs have emigrated to overseas countries to better their standard of living. As a consequence, the power structure in the village has changed and there is an embryonic formation of social class – albeit an 'Avatar of caste'. Highly educated Dalits, who hold or have held professional positions, send their children to private schools, own *pucka* houses, have access to senior district officer positions, and belong to the new emerging middle class. But it must be emphasized that they are a tiny proportion of the total population. The majority of the middle class still consists of people from the Jat Sikh families who still own all the farm land. The vast majority of Dalits still come under the category of working class (3b, 4 and 5 of Registrar General's Classification). In other words the newly emerging class hierarchy is similar to the existing caste hierarchy, with slight changes. It is clear from the interview data that micro-level social changes do and can take place when several factors coalesce, namely, educated leadership, numerical strength, enforcement of equality laws, economic independence, and progressive socio-political ethos.[18]

It became manifestly clear that there is an underlying tension between the two communities, but it is tempered by a common sense pragmatism, viz, 'we are obliged to live together in a village so let us make the most of it'. There is another factor which tones down the fractious situation between the two communities. Senior Dalits in the village are tolerant and even forgiving in their attitude to the farmers. They put down their hurts and pains due to the prevailing *zeitgeist* of the past times.

In the same vein, the senior farmers in the village are willing to accept evolving social and political changes in the village, as they realize that village polity is just a reflection of the radical political and economic changes taking place at a macro level of the Punjabi society brought about by the Dalit movements in India lead by Ambedkhar, Kanshi Ram, and Mangoo Ram.[19]

Summary

This case study was undertaken in the light of previous research and literature on Dalits which concluded that caste remains an important force/dimension in the social and personal lives of Indians. We set out to find out how the social, religious, and socio-economic positions of Dalits, especially of women, have changed since the mid-1950s in a Punjabi village. Data were collected by semi-structured interviews, participant observation, and notes from a personal diary were used to supplement this qualitative data. From the data we have ample evidence to infer that caste still impacts and shapes in a major way the social and personal lives of people in the village under study. There are separate *gurdwaras* for the Jat Sikhs and Ad Dharmis; and Valmiki families have their own *bhavan*. There are

---

18   The governments at provincial and central levels have a number of Dalit ministers who are pressing for equality and economic advancement. In addition, as discussed in the last chapter, Dalit leaders such as Mayawati are a source of great inspiration.

19   Readers are reminded that this is a case study of one village and its findings cannot be extrapolated to other villages in the Punjab or India. However, it does demonstrate that social changes do take place if important socio-economic and educational factors come together. Jodhka (2004) found a similar pattern in his large-scale study.

two cemeteries in the village: one for the Jat Sikhs and other for the Dalits. There have been no inter-caste marriages in the village and social mixing is kept to the minimum and only takes place on special occasions.

However, unlike in the 1950s, Dalits are in majority and control the village socio-political affairs through the *Panchayat* – a village council. Ritual untouchability – a common practice in the 1950s – has completely disappeared. There are no separate wells or residential areas. The village Dalits no longer work as farm labourers but seek employment in government sponsored projects and in nearby city mills. This has enhanced their self-image and boosted their morale and motivation and they are challenging the hegemony of Jat Sikhs in the village affairs. The latter are in minority and in a weak position due to the large-scale emigration of their progeny to overseas countries. There is a rising middle class of Dalits, albeit in an embryonic form.

There has been a sea-change in the lives and treatment of Dalit women. They are no longer exploited by the village farm owners, and sexual abuse, which was common in the 1950s, has completely ceased.

Chapter 4
Family, Social and Religious Organization of Dalits

We set out to find out how the family,[1] kinship, and *biraderi* play their pivotal role in the reproduction, maintenance, and renewal of the caste system in the UK. To this end, we studied five families over a protracted period of time (three years) and interviewed ten men and eight women of different castes. The extended family and *biraderi* carry on with the caste traditions; therefore, we describe in some detail the networking of Dalit families. We also discuss value-orientation and child-rearing practices of Dalits, inter-caste relationships, and social mixing amongst the Indian diaspora.

Caste division and its hierarchical structure is based on the Hindu religion's key elements of purity and pollution and sustained by the twin notions of *karma* and *dharma* as discussed in Chapter 2 of the book. Therefore Hindu temples from which Untouchables were barred until circa 1950s played a key role in preserving caste boundaries. I visited Dalit temples several times in the English Midlands and observed their mode of worship, and interviewed priests and others involved in the management. There is a detailed discussion in this chapter on the religious places of worship of Dalits and their role in reinforcing and maintaining caste divisions. A brief description of the five families who were interviewed is presented prior to detailed discussion.

First Family

This is a couple in their forties with an adolescent boy and university-educated girl. They were married over 25 years ago and live in a detached house in a better part of a city. X used to work in a factory but after redundancy payment, he has started running a taxi service. He finds his work satisfying and is content with his social and financial position. His wife is a homemaker and suffers from minor health problems. X migrated to this country when he was in his teens and attended secondary school for two years and then worked in a factory for a number of years. He is very proud of his ancestry, and the family visit India frequently to renew their social bonds and to help their kinsfolk. Their daughter has recently

---

1 Arranged endogamous marriages play an important role in maintaining caste boundaries (Dhanda, 2009). We discuss inter-caste marriages in the next chapter where the views of young people are also included.

graduated from a local university and is going to be married with an educated professional man from within their own *biraderi*. The couple's son has attended a highly acclaimed academic grammar school and is now studying at a university.[2] Their social networkings are within their community of Chamars and they go to a religious place (*bhavan*) run by their community. Their social life is conducted within their own *biraderi*.

Second Family

A single parent (Mother) is the head of her household and lives in a council house in an inner-city area. Her grandparents emigrated to the UK in 1955, therefore she is a third-generation parent. She has an adolescent boy and two girls. She has been divorced for ten years. Both her daughters left school at the age of 16 and one of them is now working in a shop. The other daughter is unemployed and is on social security benefits. Her son is at school but she does not know a great deal about his school or out-of-school activities. She told me that she was a very bad tempered and angry person prior to embracing Christianity ten years ago. She goes to a local Pentecostal church where she meets people from diverse ethnic backgrounds. Her social life revolves around her church and she has never bothered about her caste. She has visited India and does not like the caste divisions, which she encountered in her ancestral village. She is very much a 'British person' in outlook, manners, use of language, and behaviour.

Third Family (Mixed)

A couple who live together who are both divorced. The woman belongs to a Chamar family and the man hails from a farming (Jat) caste. They have both retired – she suffers from ill health and is on social security payments. She has recently converted to Christianity. Her belief is that Jesus will cure all her ill health and social problems. They mix freely with Indians of all castes and families from other ethnic backgrounds. The man's outlook is very cosmopolitan and he has never considered caste and religion as a basis for friendship or relationships. The woman used to go to a Chamar temple (*bhavan*) but did not find any spiritual or social benefits, therefore she embraced Christianity. Their children from previous marriages, have left home and they do not have any children as a couple. Recently they split up but it is not due to caste-related matters. Details of this woman also appear in Appendix A, Case Study no. 5.

---

2   Family members were interviewed three times over a period of three years. Therefore the description of the young people in the family has altered in that the girl has graduated and the boy began his university studies in 2009.

Fourth Family

This couple has been married for over 20 years and live in a very nice part of a large city. The husband works in a social services department and the wife is a homemaker. They have four daughters and one son. They both belong to the Mazhabi Sikh community. The husband is a second-generation Indian and his wife is from the Punjab and belongs to a Sikh family (See Appendix A, Case Study no. 4).

Fifth Family

This couple hails from Mazhabi families and are professionals with a son and three daughters. They live in a very good part of a large city and play a leading role in their community's affairs. I interviewed the youngest daughter, who is in the sixth form (age 16+), for over an hour and she says that she has not met caste prejudice in her school and is treated like any other Asian student. The boy has a similar view on caste. The mother teaches in a school and is of the view that caste was never an issue when she was a teenager some 25 years ago, but now it has surfaced especially where the majority of students are of Indian origin. The father is very radical on caste issues and wants to 'abolish'[3] the caste system. He has encountered prejudice from his fellow Indians at work, though he is in a managerial position. He has successfully mobilized the South Asian community's support to include caste discrimination in the Single Equality Bill (more on this in a later section of this chapter).

Immigration to the UK

Emigration from India commenced on a large scale in the 1950s and 1960s and continued until late 1970s when strict restrictions on Commonwealth citizens were imposed. Stories of these immigrants have appeared in numerous books and journals (Ghuman, 1994; Anwar, 1979; Shaw, 2000). However, no one has paid any attention to the plight of Dalit immigrant communities who have faced caste prejudice and discrimination in India and who felt marginalized from the mainstream society. Most of the Dalits in Indian villages are poor – unlike the Jat farmers who have migrated in large numbers – and secondly even when they could afford to undertake the journey overseas they faced additional hurdles. A story of a Dalit who retired after some 40 years of active business life sheds some light:

---

3   There has been a great deal of debate over the use of this term. It is argued that you can try to abolish untouchability through law and social disapproval but the caste system cannot be abolished as it is like abolishing Sufism – an Islamic sect.

> When I decided to emigrate, I needed a passport and it was a big problem. I approached a well-known Dalit minister in the Punjab and asked if he could help me. Otherwise, I had no chance. He asked me whether my family and my community have voted for him and so on ... . I vowed that that was the case and I would continue to support him. He called his PA and told him that this is an urgent case and he should approach the passport office immediately and secure a passport for me ...

A Dalit executive officer issued hundreds of passports to fellow Dalits in north India who wanted to migrate to the UK and other countries (Juergensmeyer, 1982). He was determined to help his underprivileged community to improve its economic status and thereby gain respect and honour.

The former British officers of the Raj sponsored some ex-army persons who served under their commands. A retired factory worker explained:

> I was a clerk in an army hospital, which was under the command of an English colonel. I wrote to him and asked him if he would sponsor me. He told me it would be difficult for you to get employment as a clerk, but there are factory jobs ... So he sponsored me and I came to D ... where I had my other relatives.

A first-generation Valmiki (65+) tells an interesting story of his early days and settlement:

> I came to this country in 1964 and have worked for 30 years in a steel mill. The rule was that a shared bed would cost you 50 pence per night and the rent for a bed was £1. The coal fire was only lit at the weekends and there was no heating during the week ... My food was very rich. I used to boil a pint of milk and dissolve a whole pound of butter in it. You needed the strength to do the heavy work [*He is going blind now due to diabetes and has had heart bypass surgery*]. We stayed and socialized with our *biraderi* but did mix with Jat Sikhs. My eldest son is a lecturer and holds a PhD and my daughter is a teacher. I am very pleased with the way things have turned out.

Chain Migration

It is now widely understood that people emigrating from a developing country to European countries and indeed to the US follow the route established by earlier immigrants (Ghuman, 1994; Anwar, 1979). The pioneering immigrants in the UK established themselves in big cities (London, Birmingham, and Glasgow) and subsequently sponsored their male family members and relatives to join them, for instance via marriage. Despite the many restrictions enforced by the successive British governments, the practice of arranged marriages continues as is illustrated by numerous caste-based advertisements in Punjabi and Hindi papers in the UK and North America (*Ajit*, *Des Pardes*, and the *Tribune*, Chandigarh). Many new aspiring young emigrants have had their marriages arranged in the UK and thus increased the number of Indian communities. This chain immigration of relatives, friends, and co-villagers has led to the formation of enclaves and networks such as those found in Southhall, London, and Handsworth, Birmingham. The essential elements of such networks are weekend visiting and attending one another's social and religious ceremonies. The studies of Anwar (1979) and Shaw (2000) describe in a vivid way that the extensive networks of Pakistani Muslims in England are maintained through the organization of family religious events such as *vartan bhangi*. Furthermore, reciprocal social visiting is considered an important part of belonging and staying connected with one's *biraderi* (kinship). Dalit communities have flourished in Southall, in the London Borough of Hounslow, in the English Midlands, and in Glasgow.

Overall Value Orientation and Family

The values and attitudes of Dalit immigrants can be fully understood if we use an overarching model of social psychology developed by Triandis (1991). The model postulates that Western societies mainly nurture and support individual orientation, whereas Eastern societies are based on collective orientation. Accordingly, people of South Asian origins stress the salience of joint family and *biraderi*, arranged marriages, and the primacy of a family's interest over that of the individual (Parekh, 1986) and the importance of *sangat* (Ghuman, 2003) in religious worship.

Like their fellow Indians, Dalits attach great importance to the traditions and values of their family and kinship groups. Shaw (2000: 155) notes in her fieldwork, 'They do not prize individuality as highly as westerns do, and for most of them the sacrifice of individuality that the culture requires is more than offset by the advantages of fulfilling one's role within the family, *biraderi* and community.' Stopes-Roe and Cochrane (1990), in a wide-ranging and in-depth study of two generations of South Asian young people with a control group of indigenous whites, conclude that British South Asians think that the interest of the family should come before that of the individual. Like most South Asian families, Dalit families are patriarchal and hierarchal, as I observed during my research. In all families, except one, men were in-charge in most aspects of life. Women's roles mainly relate to domestic responsibility and child-rearing. Other aspects of family life such as child-rearing, marriage arrangement, kinship relationships, are very close to other Indian groups in the UK. We now turn to the child raising practices of Dalit Punjabis.

Generational Changes in Child-rearing of Punjabis

In a comprehensive study of two generations of Punjabi parents belonging to the Sikh, Muslim, and Hindu religions (which included Dalit parents), my colleague and I (Dosanjh and Ghuman, 1996, 1997, 1997) found some very illuminating points which are relevant to understanding the social position of Dalits in the UK. We found third-generation Punjabi children were becoming increasingly English-speaking despite their parents' attempts to maintain their mother tongue. Many of them were bilingual, although only at the spoken level in their mother tongue. The presence of grandparents was helping to maintain community languages, as was the establishment of weekend schools at mosques, *mandirs*, and *gurdwaras*. Due to deep cuts in education, supporting community languages and a hope of including minority languages in the primary school curriculum was dashed. The practice of including minority languages in the formal school curriculum varies a great deal between European countries, but the psychological benefits to children of bilingualism cannot be overstated (Jones and Ghuman, 1995).

Second-generation parents have changed their attitude on giving their children freedom to choose clothes, books, and toys. As regards educational attitudes, we found that second-generation parents are more 'in tune with' the English system of education. Their attitude towards girls' education is more positive and parents and older siblings (also found in the present study) help young people with homework. The main reason for this change is that nearly all the mothers themselves have been to a school in the UK and realize the importance of active parental support.

Education researchers (Tomlinson, 1998; Verma and Ashworth, 1986; Bhachu, 1985) have found that most Indian parents have high aspirations for their children. We found similar results with our present sample of Dalit parents.[4] It is also important to note that high expectations of students are independent of social class and caste of parents.

Most parents in the 1996 study stressed the importance of religion in their family's lives and expressed a deep desire to pass it on to their children. I found a similar attitude amongst the parents in the present sample. For most Dalit parents, religion is the key element upon which their personal identities are formed and nurtured, but they are conscious of the fact that their children are going to live and work in Britain and will require the skills and values of the host society.

Most Indian parents are moving away from the strict orthodox custom of arranged marriages and are allowing their young people a degree of freedom to choose partners from within their own caste and religion. A researcher from Newcastle (Pande, 2009: 41–2) found that there are several different types of arranged marriages to be found among the young people of Indian ancestry. They range from strictly arranged to maximum freedom given to young people to date and discuss matters with parents … .

Parents in our study (Dosanjh and Ghuman, 1996) were realistic about the degree of racism their children are going to encounter in their adult lives. Their attitudes are similar to other Punjabis and Indians, many of whom prepare their children by coaxing them to study hard and obtain professional qualifications, which would secure them good jobs. It has been noted by many researchers

---

4   Details are discussed in Chapter 6.

(Verma and Ashworth, 1986; Smith and Tomlinson, 1989) that a common refrain among parents is: 'You have to be twice as good as your white peers to compete successfully in the job market.'

Most Indian parents accept the developing biculturalism and dual identities of their children and are prepared to change their own life styles and outlook (Stopes-Roe and Cochrane, 1991). In doing so, they are trying to fuse the two differing value systems which they can then pass on to their progeny.

Places of Worship

All South Asian immigrant communities have raised funds to establish their respective places of worship. Major cities in the UK have Hindu temples, Sikh *gurdwaras*, Muslim mosques, and Buddhist *viharas*. A detailed account of their efforts has appeared in many books and monographs but we present a short resume of the struggle of Dalits to raise their own *bhavans*, *viharas*, and *gurdwaras*.

Ballard (1994:110) writes:

> Thus even though the division of labour which underpinned the caste hierarchy has virtually disappeared in Britain, caste remains a vitally important vehicle for community and religious organisation ... In most British towns with a significant Sikh population one finds a plethora of rival gurdwaras, each with a caste-specific management committee.

Singh and Tatla (2006: 77–9) describe in detail the position of lower-caste (Untouchable) Sikhs. They argue that Ravidasis and Valmikis[5] want to develop their own distinctive 'religious' identities that are separate and distinctive both from Sikh and Hindus religions. Discussion on this issue is to be found later in this chapter.

In London, Birmingham, Coventry, Wolverhampton, Glasgow, and other major cities and towns of Indian immigrant settlements there are temples of Ravidasi and Valmiki communities. The existence of separate *gurdwaras* and Hindu temples reinforce the institution of caste and secure its continual significance. A Jat Sikh respondent argued:

> Now we have *gurdwaras* along the caste lines; Jats (farmers) were the first followed by Ramgharias (carpenters), and lastly the Chamars (Ravidasis) all have separate places. What is the point? The Sikh gurus forbade caste distinctions but it has crept back in our religion.

---

5   The authors mention 13 *bhavans* and nine Valmiki 'places of worship' in England alone. The question whether the majority of Ravidasis still consider themselves Sikhs is yet to be ascertained by empirical research because of the new-found confidence of this community in the UK and India (see Chapters 1 and 7 for extended discussion).

Shaw (2000) also notes that Muslims in Oxford widely uphold caste distinctions widely when inviting people for marriages, Khatimini Koran (full recitation of the Koran), and other social engagements, though they are forbidden from maintaining a caste system.[6]

Now we describe the opinions and attitudes of our respondents on this important issue. A Ravidasi woman (child-care worker 30+) described to me to an incident which was repeated many times over during my fieldwork:

> This woman was in a local *gurdwara* taking part in the Sunday service and worship. After the *bhog* ceremony *parsad* is distributed and this woman offered her services, as the lay people normally do … She was stopped and told she cannot perform this duty because she is a Chamari i.e. [belongs to an Untouchables caste who were traditionally leather workers and are considered to be polluting].

Likewise, many other incidents were related which revealed a derogatory and insulting attitude of high-caste Sikhs to Dalit worshippers. A successful Dalit businessman (age 65+) recounted:

> The Jats [farmers] only tolerate you as long as you are a quiet member of the *Sangat* [congregation], but if you want to have your voice heard, then forget it and look out. They will throw you out. The old caste prejudice comes to the surface … They never forget that they were the *sardars* [chiefs] in Punjabi villages and we were farm labourers, which amounted to no more than bonded labour … It is not the Brahmins who suppressed us but the Jat community (see Chapter 3 for details).

Jats Sikh interviewees in our research expressed their views candidly on caste prejudice. Some acknowledged that there are a few cases of prejudice and discrimination and they very much regret it, because this is against the teaching of Sikh gurus. However, some argued that the Ravidas community wants to assert its separate identity by building separate temples. A Jat teacher's comment (age 45+) makes it clear:

> In our holy book, *Guru Granth Sahib*, there are hymns of our Gurus and 24 *bhagats* [saints] of other castes and religions, including Shri Ravidas ji. But they want to give prime importance to Guru Ravidas whereas we respect him as a *bhagat* but not one of the Gurus … Although they have the *Guru Granth Sahib* in their places of worship, some of them like to call it Ravidas *Bhavan* [more like a Hindu temple] and also to have their Nishan Sahib (a tall flag pole) different

---

6   Readers interested in caste issues amongst British Pakistani Muslims are referred to Shaw's excellent book (2000: Chapters 4 and 5).

to the one adopted by the Shri Guru Prabandhak Committee [management] at Amritsar ... So we say, you go your own way but we can still be a fraternity.

A former president of Guru Ravidas Bhavan (age 63+) narrated stories of caste discrimination and concluded:

> I would say that we all contributed to build new *gurdwaras* in the 1960s in good faith but were disappointed that we were treated as second class citizens ... Nobody from our community was on management committees and there were other incidents of discrimination and insults, so we decided to go our own way ... I would say Jats should take this responsibility ... I retired a few years ago and I am invited to parties where high-caste peoples' attitude makes me uncomfortable so I do not go. It is very disappointing as I was a *pucka* Sikh [he showed me his photograph with full beard and turban to prove it] and Sikhism preaches equality ...

However, the position of the Valmiki community is different from the Ravidas community. Traditionally they used to be called by derogatory names and had a lower status in the Doab area of the Punjab[7] than the other Untouchables such as Chamars because they were sweepers, cowshed cleaners, and night soil collectors. However, it is widely understood and strongly advocated by the community that *rishi*/saint Valmiki was an Untouchable who wrote the *Ramayana*, the sacred book of the Hindus. Not only did he write the holy book but also supported and nurtured two sons and the wife (Sita) of Lord Rama when they were in exile. The story goes that Lord Rama exiled his wife and sons because he mistakenly believed that Sita was not virtuous and worthy of being a queen. Bhagwan Valmiki made Rama recant his wrongdoing and restored the unity of the family. Therefore, it is argued that far from being Untouchables they are closely associated with the Hindu pantheon and originally belonged to the Kshatriya (high) caste. They also claim a place of high status and prestige within the Sikh religion as Baba Deep Singh of the Valmiki was one of the army chiefs of Maharaja Ranjit Singh. Furthermore, another notable Sikh (Bhai Jivan Singh) risked his life in bringing the slain body of the ninth Sikh guru from Delhi to the Punjab and earned the accolade of 'a distinguished son of Sikhs'. During the British Raj, military authorities saw fit to form separate regiments of Valmiki Sikhs because they were known for their valour and integrity.

To assert their identity and independence from high-caste Hindus and Sikhs they have established Valmiki *bhavans* where the holy book is Valmiki's *Ramayana*. A Valmiki factory manager's (age 45+) comment illustrates the point:

> I immigrated to this country in April 1980. At that time, there was no *bhavan* in our city where our community could go and worship. There were Hindu temples

---

7   Districts Jallander and Hoshiarpur of the Punjab.

and Sikh *gurdwaras* but we were not welcomed there … I happened to be on the city planning committee, which gives grants to the local community. I pleaded a case for an award. There was a great deal of sympathy for our cause, and we were successful in obtaining a large grant. … Now it is a fine place for our people to meet, pray and we teach our children.

In our earlier research (Thomas and Ghuman, 1976), we found that Bhatras, who are considered low-caste Sikhs in Cardiff, have built a separate *gurdwara* for their community and want to retain control of it by excluding Jat and Ramgarhia from the management committee, though it is open to all for worship.

A research report by Kalsi (1992: 38) deals with caste divisions within Sikhism. His empirical research was carried out in Leeds and Bradford, England, and furthermore he analysed the existing literature on caste amongst Sikhs and concludes: 'Although relatively few in number, these studies provide much empirical evidence to refute the view that the Sikhs are a casteless brotherhood, according to their teaching they profess to be.'

Guru Ravidas Bhavan: A Case Study

This *bhavan* in Birmingham was founded in 1997 with the help of collections from ordinary members of the Ravidas community in the city and surrounding areas. This is like any other Sikh *gurdwara* to be found in Britain's main cities in that it is entirely financed and run by the community. There is no central authority, which controls their mode and style of worship. The main congregation takes place in a very large hall which is carpeted for the *sangat* to sit on. The hall is decorated with pictures of Guru Ravidas, Guru Nanak, Bhagat Kabir, Baba Farid, and other saints, but not of Guru Gobind Singh, the tenth and last guru of the Sikhs. This is a significant omission. He baptized Sikhs to form the Khalsa, which became an exclusive community and did not include 'others'. At one end of the hall is a raised dais for the holy book (*Guru Granth Sahib*) which is draped in silk sheets and scarves and is attended by a priest who abides by the Sikh dress code (uncut beard and turban) and refrains from smoking and drinking. The holy book is composed of *shabads* and *slokas* (hymns) of Sikh gurus and 16 *bhagats* (saints)[8] one of whom is Shri Guru Ravidas Ji . During a service or a wedding ceremony, women and men sit separately on the carpets but they can sit as a family (mixed) when taking meals at the *gurdwara*. No smoking and drinking is allowed in the *gurdwara*. There are free meals available (*langar*) at lunch and dinnertime and this proves very attractive to pensioners and unemployed people. The *bhavan* also runs a Sunday school where Guru Ravidas Ji's life story and teachings are taught as well as Punjabi. The *bhavan* is run by a democratically elected committee and

---

8   For details see Singh (1999: 306).

elections are held every five years. I interviewed the president of the *bhavan* and his remarks are worth quoting:

> Our *bhavan* is like a Sikh *gurdwara* and is run along similar lines to Sikhs' except that it is controlled by our community. Some *bhavans* are run like Hindu temples in that there are statutes of deities and the services are closer to those of Hindu temples ... I think the Sikh gurus forbade caste distinctions and discriminations so we are closer to them in our religious philosophy. I also realize that caste consciousness is to be found amongst many Sikhs but many Hindus still actively justify the origins and merits of the caste system. [He cited the recent controversy on caste to support his claim – my comments].

There is one significant theological point which separates this temple from high-caste Sikh *gurdwaras*. In the final prayer, prominence is given to Guru Ravidas Ji and the final recitation is in his name rather than the traditional Sikh prayer.

In some *bhavans*, eminent Dalit saints from India preside over the services. They symbolically sit at the same level as the holy book to show their spiritual equality to the Sikh gurus, which has caused a great deal of friction between Ravidasi Sikhs and the mainstream Sikhs. A former president of this *bhavan* (age 63+) told me:

> We used to have a saint from India who presided over the Sunday *bhog* ceremonies and collect money from the *sangat* for building temples and hospitals in the Punjab. People gave generously and he took money by the bucketfuls but there was no accountability. When I became president, I stopped all that and drew a new constitution, which forbade such practices. Our services are now very close to traditional Sikh services.

Valmiki Bhavan[9]

Like other South Asian communities, Valmikis[10] are a small but close-knit community who have built their temples for worship, social networking, and political mobilization. This temple was built seven years ago[11] by putting two

---

9   For details see Nesbitt's ethnographic study (1994).

10   The followers of Bhagwan Valmiki are called Valmikis. Leslie (2003: 160–95) presents a very lucid and detailed account of the Valmiki religious and social movement. She says Bahgwan Valmiki was considered a holy man – a deity (Visnu in human form) in seventh-century Campa culture. She quotes Valmiki Jagriti (vol. 2, 4) to describe the principles of the religion: 'not gambling, not stealing, and not exploiting the poor; and meditation as the path towards understanding oneself.'

11   This group split from the mainstream Valmikis who have their temple in the city centre in an old primary school building. The president of this temple explained to me that

adjacent houses together to make provisions for: keeping the holy book in one room, a communal kitchen, a dining hall, and a reception room. The congregation of this *bhavan* is rather small compared to the Guru Ravidas temple described in the preceding section. *Sangat* shows its solidarity by attending services on Sunday where announcements are made of important social occasions such as weddings and engagements and forthcoming political meetings. Services are conducted by reading from the Valmiki *Ramayana* and singing or narrating the exploits and good deeds of their saints. In addition to *rishi*/saint Valmiki they also worship Guru Gian Nath ji.

Close to the room where the holy book is kept for services, I noticed a fully furnished bedroom with a washbasin where their chief deity is supposed to rest. According to their belief, their saint is a 'living' being who needs a room to rest and sleep. This shows a clear influence of Hinduism on their worshipping mode and elevates their caste status from Untouchables to the higher caste of Kshatriya – the warrior caste.[12] All over the temple there are pictures of Valmiki and other saints, Hindu gods, and Guru Nanak (the founder of Sikh religion). In the dining hall there are leaflets on a variety of social and cultural activities arranged by the *bhavan*'s official and information on the forthcoming events concerning the Valmiki community locally and in the UK.

The community are thinking of introducing a programme for the young children which may include the teaching of religion and Punjabi. There is an on-going programme of extending the temple complex to accommodate to the social and cultural needs of the community. The management committee is collecting donations from their devotees and have applied to the local authority for financial assistance. One of their priests is from a nearby city. He has a flowing beard and sports a turban (as do a few other devotees) and looks like a *bhai* (priest) of a mainstream Sikh *gurdwara*. His surname is a common Jat Sikh caste name in the Punjab. I had a long conversation with him and gathered the impression that he is synthesizing the essential elements of Sikhism and Hinduism but at the same time constructing and forging a distinctive identity for his Valmiki community.

A young girl (nurse, age 23+) who is going to run the Sunday school told me her story which illuminates some of the points raised in this chapter. The following summary is from my notes.

> When she qualified as a nurse her uncle said to her why do you not try to become a doctor? Being a nurse you will get your hands dirty.[13] She is a strong-minded

---

for them there is not one but two holy *rishis* to worship: Valmiki and Gian Nath.

12   This strategy of elevating caste status is described by Srinivas (2000) as 'Sanskritization', that is, improving caste status by copying the rituals and practices of high castes.

13   Valmikis are still very conscious that in the eyes of high-caste people they are sweepers and collectors of night soil. They want to overcome this stigma in the UK (see Nesbitt, 2000). In north India the majority of hospital nurses and auxiliaries used to be from

girl and said no; I like to be a nurse. She is now spearheading a programme for the younger generation. Her father helps with the services and they are determined to build 'caste pride' in their community's children. Her British education has been very good and she has never come across any caste prejudice in school. She has never been to India, yet. She says: 'we are Chamars and Churas but we are proud of it. In this country all communities are treated equally and this is not so in India.' Valmikis have a big *bhavan* in Southhall and they have played their part in building it. Some members of their community in north India have converted to Christianity to escape the stigmatism associated with their Untouchable caste.

Temples and Education

All the *gurdwaras* and temples play (or aspire to play) a role in imparting the rudiments of the community's religion to its children and young people. A Valmiki community leader's comments are illuminating:[14]

> This is one of the important things we want to do ... I have asked M to look after this aspect of the work. We intend to hold classes where we will teach the basic tenets of our religion so that our children are proud of their inheritance and root them into its philosophy ... There are problems of books and other material but we are working on it.

Likewise, a president of Guru Ravidas Bhavan was convinced on the role of weekend classes to teach children the basics of Guru Ravidas's ideas and to teach Punjabi.

Most of the parents interviewed for this research are Punjabis and therefore speak Punjabi at home. It is refreshing to note that they are very keen that their children should learn Punjabi and frequently use it at home and on social occasions. This is an interesting feature to note because they do not think that Punjabi is a low status language, like Hindu Punjabis from India and Muslim Punjabis from Pakistan. Some of their responses are given below.

A part-time teacher (aged 45+) remarks:

---

the Valmiki community, and they were undertaking tasks which were/are considered to be polluting, that is, washing and dressing the wounds of patients and helping them in their personal hygiene.

14   In my experience, most Hindus want to teach Hindi rather than Punjabi to their children for reasons which are too complex to deal with in this text. Briefly, they think it is useful as a spoken language, and for learning their religious texts it is Hindi which is needed. Also, as a national language of India it enjoys a higher status. Pakistani Punjabi Muslims feel the same way about Urdu.

There is a sort of imperialism about Asian languages. Most Muslim parents think that Urdu is the best language to learn – [it is derived from Arabic and is associated with the Moguls who were rulers of India for several centuries] though they speak Punjabi at home. Likewise, Hindus feel about Hindi ... Punjabi is largely promoted by the Sikhs, Ad Dharmis and Valmikis – these Punjabi communities think this is the language of the masses in Punjab and feel it is their mother tongue and an authentic vehicle for communication.

Parents interviewed from other communities, for example, Gujarati and Bengali also favour, the retention of their respective mother tongues. However, it seems from the literature (Smith and Tomlinson, 1989) that Muslim parents are more determined than other religious communities to teach their mother tongues. Two noted scholars (Smith and Tomlinson, 1989) argue for the retention of community language:

> One of the most important steps that schools can take towards a multicultural education policy is to develop the teaching of Asian languages and literature within the framework of the national Curriculum.

Inter-caste Relations

One of the major aims of this book is to explore inter-caste relationships through protracted observations and in-depth interviews. We report here perceptions and views of Dalit and higher-caste people on this topic.

A high-caste businessman (age 67+) expressed his strongly held views of the Dalit communities:

> They (Dalits) suffer from the same complex of persecution and victimization as they do in India. Many of them hold good jobs but they break the law. They abbreviate their names so that they cannot be identified. A lot of them have become Bodis (Buddhists) but do not know anything about its principles. They curse Hindu gods Rama and Krishna. ... That is why high-caste people do not want to mix with them. Their young people do not make the most of the opportunities offered. A large number drift into criminal activities. Parents never go to schools when there is an open day partly because they do not know how to conduct themselves. Therefore it is their own weakness that they fall behind other castes; but they blame others.

A high-caste young professional's (age, 25+) views are close to the above:

> In India, there is no pressure on them to work in dirty jobs; it is their choice. Education is free and there is job 'reservations'. In my judgement, 30 per cent of Dalits suffer from persecution complex. In this country, they still harp on the

caste inequality. In my view, some caste consciousness may be there but younger people are free from this and are marching ahead ... Marriages are within caste and so is the social mixing. That will take time to change.

It is difficult to generalize but the above two interviewees do reflect the attitude of many orthodox high-caste people. As we found in the last chapter, many Jats blame Dalits for their poor socio-economic conditions. Reasons given to support such a contention run like this: 'They are lazy, spend time drinking and smoking, and the successive governments have spoilt them.' This style of rationalization is termed as 'blaming the victim' for their predicament by negatively stereotyping the whole community. In the US, racists have argued that the segregation of African-Americans, and their all-round poor social and economic situation was because of their 'low intelligence and poor motivation'. Some psychologists (Eysenck, 1971) supported this contention by linking it to genetic factors.

Allport (1954: 191) defines a stereotype as 'Whether favourable or unfavourable a stereotype is an exaggerated belief associated with a category. Its function is to justify our conduct in relation to that category.' Allport argues that stereotypes should not be confused with 'categories', which are there to describe our social world. However, contemporary interpretation is somewhat mixed in that they both are thought to serve the same purpose of simplifying our perception and thinking about the social world (see Leyens et al., 1994; Davey, 1983). The formation and continuance of negative stereotypes is due to prejudice in the first instance, argues Allport. Providing young people with objective information about a group (for example, caste, immigrants, and gender) can slowly change a 'negative' outlook into a positive one.

A recent report by Sharma (2008) comes close to justifying caste (without untouchability) and suggests that it is akin to social class in the UK and other Western countries. He asserts that his is the authentic interpretation of the holy texts such as the *Bhagavad Gita* and *Manusmriti*. According to the author, foreign scholars with little knowledge of the original Sanskrit texts have misunderstood the *varna* system and mislead people into believing that it is an evil system (A detailed analysis of the report is to be found in Chapter 2 (pages 26–8).

A Dalit woman (age 55) expressed her views:

First generation were very keen to retain caste loyalties, but the younger generation do not care. There are several cases of Chamar boys marrying Jat girls. In India, it is also happening because Chamars are well off and own property and have good jobs. ... Many Dalits in this country are embracing Christianity because it is free of the caste system. In Christianity, they do care for you unlike in *gurdwaras*, Hindu temples and *bhavan*s where you prepare food for people ...

This interviewee also mentioned that many Dalits find Christianity very attractive: 'They genuinely care for all their followers unlike our places of worships where women are confined to making *langar* (communal meals) for the *Sangat*.' She was of the view that in Christianity you find all ethnic groups and nationalities whereas our people are narrow and bigoted. I found a similar situation in the US where many Indians are embracing Christianity (Ghuman, 2003).

A successful Valmiki retired businessperson (age 67+) described his feelings:

> We work hard and have good relations with the Ravidasi community, but Jats and Brahmins do not cooperate with us. They feel jealous of our success in this country. ... Brahmins have to change their attitudes – they poison (and muddy the waters of) relationships because of their belief in the caste system. They teach their children the same nonsense of caste superiority and say to them: 'Do not eat with the Untouchables because they are not clean!' Hindus and Sikhs distort the facts and preach hatred against us in their temples and *gurdwaras* ... Route to understanding is through education ... By the by I have converted to Buddhism.

This man's son is a teacher and runs very successful night classes for Indian children who want to sit the selective examination at (11+). His grandchildren go to private schools and he is a passionate advocate of developing Dalit identity based on the ideas of Baba Sahib Ambedkar.

A significant minority of Dailts in the UK (Dalit Solidarity Network: website 2006) do not wish to engage in caste controversy or make it a big issue for their children.

A successful Dalit businessman's (age 50+) response illustrates the point:

> I am opening two stores in the Punjab. All my family is professional – lawyers, judges, and doctors. We are well placed, confident and successful and do not care about the 'ignorant' people who still practise caste discrimination. Our *bhavans* are open to all and we teach Punjabi to children on weekends.

Here is a lengthy quote from a discussion which I had with a group of five young people (age 25 years+ all Dalits and Bodis):

> Caste divisions are alive and kicking 'back at home' and here in England. It is a part of Indian people's psyche. In *gurdwaras*, people always ask your caste or sub-caste to establish their superiority. In principle, Sikh religion prohibits caste divisions but in practice it is not any different from Hindus and Muslims. Buddhists preach equality whereas other religions preach class and caste divisions. ... My daughter met 'caste attitudes' at school and it became more marked when she was in college, and I had a similar experience. ... Valmiki *bhavans* are OK but they are going the wrong way. They are participating in the Hindu system by believing that Guru Valmiki wrote the Hindu holy book [*Ramayana*] and he was closely associated with Sita [wife of God Rama] and her boys. Our situation is worse than that of Blacks in America. We cannot sit at the same table as blacks do with whites. That is why we believe in Dr

Ambedkar's policy of 'educate, agitate, and unite'. Baba Sahib Ambedkar was not against high-caste people but against Brahmanism, which is based on caste hierarchy, empty rituals, and exclusion.

These young people were very articulate, knowledgeable and had created national and international networks to mobilize Dalit community to improve the desperate positions of their people in India.

Dalit Christians from India have immigrated to the UK in small numbers and their experience of living in Britain is very positive as is testified by a Dalit taxi driver (age 50+).

> We do not face any problem with caste but there is a stigma attached to being Christian in the Indian community. Indian people are more racist than whites. When I was young in India we were walking back from school on a very hot day. My mate wanted to have a drink from the well but the farmer stopped him and said: 'Go and drink down the watering little stream (this is where the farm animals drink from!). This incident has stuck in my mind and ever since then I do not wish to go back to India ... Our community is very hardworking who care for their children's education and make many sacrifices. Our younger generation is doing well and that is a matter of great satisfaction.

However, Christian Dalits from Pakistan have harrowing stories to tell of harassment, murder, and police framing. A priest (age 40+) who has settled in England told me of his experiences:

> A couple quarrelled over a minor matter and the wife burnt a copy of the Koran and then made a big fuss. The villagers burnt the husband alive because she alleged that it is her husband who has done it. There are grave injustices in our society in which Dalits are treated as serfs and servants. Once with the aid and collaboration of police they burnt the whole village because they alleged villagers have blasphemed against the prophet Mohammed. I am trained as a nurse but I am going to be ordained soon and then I can be a part-time preacher.

Regrettably, I could manage to interview only six women individually. The reason for this is now well understood, namely the patriarchal nature of the Indian families who still believe that a man should be the spokesperson for the whole family. The following are comments of a very confident Dalit homemaker (age 40+) which throw some light on caste relationships:

> When I was at school, we were all Asians and this is 20 years ago. No Asian boys and girls bothered us about our caste but it has come into prominence now. There are many more *gurdwaras* and temples now and they have made Indian people aware of their castes. However, the younger generation are 'marrying inter-caste' because they are aware of their rights in this country, so the caste

system should fade away. In this country, the stress is on individual's rights and not on the family as we used to do.

A Dalit woman teacher (age 35+) agreed with the above interviewee:

> When I was growing up 25 years ago *gurdwaras* were not divided and we were all together. People used to say it does not matter – values were different then. Now they ask you where are you from? Then they work it out that you belong to an Untouchable caste. To the British we are all blacks or Pakis ... Books on the caste system should be replaced and a fairer version should be written to give a broader perspective. The caste system should be condemned as unjust in this age and in this location [meaning the UK].

Her visiting woman relative from Indian made a very interesting comment:

> In India, in big cities no body bothers about your caste. It is more prominent here. *Gurdwaras* are along caste line but I do not feel that way in the Punjab or Delhi ... My relatives are mixed: some are Mazhabi Sikhs, others are Valmikis and some have converted to Christianity ...

The treasurer (age 35+) of a Ravidas *gurdwara* was very optimistic about the future of his community:

> Jat girls are marrying Chamar boys and we are happy to perform the wedding ceremony. It is young people's choice and they have spoken against their parents ... Sikh religion tells us to respect all, but Jat people misinterpret it. It is due to jealousy, nothing else, in my view. We do our job and work hard. We do not owe anything to Jats or others so they should not boss us. This is about dominance and *Chowder* [Power]. We do not tell our children that they are Chamars, as we do not want to burden them with extra problems. The same blood flows through our veins. My son did ask me once and I said we are Sikhs – a religion in which everyone is equal.

However, there are many parents who openly accept their caste ties and are proud of them. A Dalit taxi driver (age 45+) had this observation to make:

> I say I am a Chamar and proud of it. Our ancestor used to work with leather – making shoes and so on. But, now in this country we do the same jobs as other caste people and our kids are doing as well as theirs in schools and obtaining good jobs ... Someone from the local *gurdwara* asked me to become a Sikh and wear long hair and turban. My response was: Would Jats then marry into my family? The answer is clearly no – so why should I change my identity?

Caste Discrimination

From the above quotes and discussion, it follows that caste prejudice is widespread amongst the Indian diaspora. The important question to ask now is whether this prejudice leads to discrimination in employment, education, and the provision of services in the UK.[15]

The Anti Caste Discrimination Alliance (ACDA, website 2009) reports the findings of a survey based on 300 respondents. The researchers used nine focus groups[16] and a comprehensive questionnaire to find out the extent and scale of caste discrimination in England and Wales. The Report does not include information on how many people were invited to take part, but 101 completed the questionnaire. The majority of the respondents were from the Ravidasi community (45 per cent), but there were no Valmikis, who are another significantly large Untouchable community. This is one of the shortcomings of the survey. An interesting point to note is that the majority (78 per cent) of the respondents were in the age range of '25–59', that is, they are in employment or seeking employment. 80 per cent of the sample said they were aware of the caste system and of their own caste. My own case study (number 4) confirms such discrimination in employment:

> I've got lots of friends across all castes – they don't seem to think I am from the Ravidasi community. They talk to me openly. I had a fellow accountant, she was trainee at the local authority and we were talking about marriage. She said: 'mum told me that I could find anybody but whatever I do, do not find a Chamar.' I just looked at her and went, 'hmmm' ...

Fifty-eight per cent of the respondents said that they have been discriminated against because of their caste, and 37 per cent of them stated that this has taken place on several occasions. The report quotes many examples of caste prejudice and some of discrimination in employment. A case study from the report is illustrative:

> Indrajit faced discrimination in his work place ... When some Asians amongst staff realised that Indrajit was a Dalit, they complained about him and brought disciplinary action against him saying he was inefficient. They also organised a protest against at the centre, upon which the management closed down the centre. It was opened after a month without Amarjit (ACDA, 2009: 21).

The authors, however, suggest that it is a preliminary study and a more rigorous study with a larger sample is required to confirm, or to refute their findings. But

---

15   There is no evidence, known to the writer, which suggests that 'indigenous' whites in the UK show caste prejudice or are even widely aware of the caste system.

16   The majority of the participants were Ravidasis, and Ambedkarites (mainly Buddhists and followers of Baba Sahib Ambedkar).

the interesting point is that Ravidasi people are not taking it lying down. There are several examples in the report of resistance:

> He thought he was superior and did not need to do as much work as me. I kept asking him: 'What do you think you are doing?' He would just shrug his shoulders. One day I had had enough and got him by the throat? What else could I do? What does he think? Chamars are not pushovers? (ACDA, 2009)

This report was submitted by 17 anti-caste associations (ACDA, website 2009) to the Committee on Equality and Human Rights Commission as evidence of caste discrimination in the UK. The aim was to urge lawmakers in the UK to include caste discrimination in the Single Equality Bill under discussion in March 2010. However, the Government was not fully convinced of the evidence presented and has commissioned its own research. The research is to be conducted by NIESR and its findings submitted to the minister concerned.[17] The advocates argue that the government has paid more heed to the 'Hindu Forum of Britain' and the 'Hindu Council UK' who contend that caste prejudice is at personal and social levels and does not affect the life chances and employment opportunities of Dalits. In sum, it is clear that the legislation on caste discrimination now depends on the findings of the commissioned report which was expected to be completed in July/August 2010.

Concluding Remarks

In the introduction to this chapter, we noted that chain migration has produced a village-like situation in many Indian settlements. This is because kith and kin have strived to live in close proximity to each other so that they can provide mutual support and engage in social networking. It is clear from our interviews and protracted observation of Dalit families that most social and neighbourly dealings still take place within caste *biraderi* amongst Indians. Shaw (2000) found a similar trend amongst Pakistanis of different castes. It is also well documented in the literature (Ghuman, 2000; Shaw, 2000) that endogamous arranged marriages

---

17   On 2 March 2010, the House of Lords voted for an amendment to the Equality bill, which, according to government minister Thorton, would 'prohibit unlawful discrimination and harassment because of caste in the same way as for colour, ethnicity, nationality and ethnic or national origins.' The UK government, however, feels that there is a need for more in-depth research on caste discrimination (ACDA, 2010). The comissioned report has just been released (Metcalf and Rolfe, 2010: vi) and it concludes: 'The study identified evidence suggesting caste discrimination and harrassment of the type covered by the Equality Act 2010 in relation to: work (bullying, recruitment, promotion, task orientation); provision of services; and education (pupil on pupil bullying).

are the norm amongst the Indian diaspora.[18] It follows that caste divisions are produced through endogamous marriages, maintained by within-caste social relationships, and reinforced by religious institutions, which are established along caste and sectarian lines. Paradoxically, Sikh *gurdwaras* were/are meant to eradicate caste consciousness through common *langar* and *pangat* arrangements, but they have become institutions through which caste boundaries are sharpened and strengthened.

Another unequivocal finding of our research is that Dalits of all political and social hues are immensely proud of their respective religion and caste and do not feel in any way inferior to Jats or Brahmins.[19] Most want a dialogue and social interchange with their fellow Indians but on equal footing. They are charitable enough to forget about the past hurts and insults showered upon them and their ancestors, but their thinking and actions are not always reciprocated by high-caste Indians. This has caused tension, quarrels, and even physical fights amongst high-caste people and Dalits.

However, it seems that many Jats and other high-caste Indians are changing their traditionally held caste attitudes positively,[20] but the process is slow and appears condescending to Dalits. There are still many diehard high-caste people in the UK who are not willing to accept a new era in inter-caste relations.

Most marriages, though not traditionally arranged, are still within caste and religion. Those young people who venture to cross the caste lines still have difficult times (see Dhanda, 2009). However, as the old traditions fade away, there is a growing number of young people who defy caste boundaries. Many young people are now third- and fourth-generation and their link with India's social and political life is becoming tenuous and/or romantic. The secular and individualist style of functioning is gradually replacing the religious and collectivist style of thinking of the first-generation. Several interviewees switched into a type of discourse which reflected this style of thinking, viz: 'it is their /our life'; 'we cater for the individual'; 'we have to respect their wishes'; and 'it is up to them'. This and other issues concerning young people are explored further in the next two chapters.

---

18 The clear evidence is to be found in Indian newspapers both in the UK and India. For example, the Sunday editions of *The Hindu*, *The Tribune*, and *The Times* carry numerous matrimonial ads along caste lines. This is also the case with Punjabi, Hindi, and English weeklies in the UK.

19 This finding is somewhat contrary to the findings of ACDA research (2009) where it is argued that many Chamars feel insulted and hurt when high caste people call them by this 'traditional name'. It is contended that 'half the respondents identified themselves as Chamars' which is an offensive and derogatory term. They surmise that this has deep roots within South Asian culture and 'many bear it as a yoke' while others make a political statement (see Dhanda, 2009 on this point). In India it is an offence to call anyone Chamar or Chura punishable by imprisonment and there is no bail (see Chapter 2).

20 The inclusion of caste in the Single Equality bill should be of great help in laying a framework of equality of opportunity.

Chapter 5
Voices of Young People

Introduction

The first generation of Indians immigrated to Britain primarily to improve their standard of living and thereby to benefit their extended families back at home. Another motive for settling in the UK was to enable their offspring to avail themselves of the excellent educational opportunities. The education system of the UK is held in very high regard primarily due to its quality. It is a world leader in several fields of learning, research, and scholarship. The eminent leader of the Dalit people, Baba Sahib Ambedkar, underlined the importance of education in the uplift of depressed castes. His slogan: 'Unite, Organize and Educate' is taken very seriously by his followers. He was a distinguished scholar who held senior doctorates from London University and the University of Columbia.

This chapter is concerned with the educational progress of Dalit students and their views on caste-related issues. It presents their views on their identities and the role of caste in their lives. Furthermore, from their interviews we present their mode of adaptation to the British way of life. Previous scholars researching the educational achievements of Indian students have not included caste as a variable. Our findings are original in the sense that we identified the caste of students and discussed its significance in their school life.

Description of Schools

Thirty boys and ten girls from two multicultural (mainly South Asian) comprehensive schools were interviewed on a one-to-one basis. Both schools are multicultural with high percentage of South Asian students. There are several ethnic minority teachers in both schools. One is a co-educational grant-maintained school with high academic standards. The second is a girls' secondary school with an average academic record. The heads of both schools are Afro-Caribbean males who are deeply committed to pursuing multicultural policies. The writer has been acquainted with both schools since the 1980s and knows the staff and school ethos well. We placed our PGCE students there for teaching practice and enjoyed good relations with the staff and successive head teachers in both schools.

Table 5.1 gives details of the sample selected for interviews. It is important to note that students for interviews were chosen by the heads. The main purpose of the research was explained to them, namely to assess students' views on caste-related matters. The heads were shown the questionnaire on which interviews were based.

They were requested to select representative samples as far as possible within the constraints of their respective schools, for example, time-tabling and exam commitments. Most of the ethnic minority teachers and head teachers in both schools were interviewed on caste issues as were three school governors to gain a broader perspective. The schools were generous in their hospitality and gave me a room for interviews and provided me with refreshments. Empirical information on our student sample and their responses on various issues are presented in Table 5.1. The boys and girls belong to mainly two castes, Jat Sikhs and Hindu and Sikh

Table 5.1   Sample description

Number of boys from school A	10	Boys from school B	0	
Number of girls from school A	7	Girls from school B	13	
Age range 12–18 years				
Total number of boys	10			
Total number of girls	20			
Caste affliation Boys:	Jats 5	Chamars 5	Ghumar 0	
Caste affiliation Girls:	Jats 10	Chamars 9	Ghumar 1	
Total	**30**			

Chamars, whose parents or grandparents emigrated from the Punjab. All the students gave their caste affiliation willingly and without hesitation (see Appendix B for the questionnaire used for the interviews).

Methodology

Students were interviewed individually in a room set aside for this purpose by head teachers. The main thrust of the interview was to learn students' opinions on the Indian caste system, and how far it affects their identity and life in school. Questions on other aspects of education are included to provide a broader context to the research. This method of collecting data has been successfully used by various scholars in their research projects (Bhatti, 1999, 1999; Verma and Ashworth, 1980) and details are to be found in my book *Double Loyalties* (Ghuman, 2003: 53). Briefly, interviews were conducted in English and on average it took 15 to 30 minutes to ask the questions. The purpose of research was explained to the students and they were happy to co-operate. They thought the project was

Table 5.2   Students' responses on caste matters

		Jats	Chamars
Caste awareness	Yes	15	15
Do parents talk about it?	Yes	15	15
Experienced name calling	Yes	0	4
Caste bullying	Yes	0	3
Caste identity	No	15	15
Proud of my caste	Yes	15	15

Table 5.3   Students' responses on educational matters

	Manual	Skilled manual	Professionals
Father's occupation	10	14	6
Mother's occupation	6	14	4 (and 6 are home makers)

	Yes	No	
Help with home work	30	–	
Computer at home	30	–	
Favourite subject	Science and maths based 19	Humanities 11	
Language spoken at home	English only 15	Punjabi only 0	Both 15
Learning Punjabi	Yes 2	No 28	
Attendance at temples	Regularly 11	On special occasions 19	
Equality of boys and girls at home	Yes 15	No 15	
Have you been back to India?	Yes 28	No 2	

Your identity

British 1	Indian 8	Asians 0	
British Asians 7	British Indian 12	Sikhs 2	

Occupation aspirations	All want to follow a professional career
Higher education	All want to attend an institution of higher education

a worthwhile attempt to improve inter-caste relations. This technique yields rich data which is extremely illuminating but it has its shortcomings. The main weakness is that only a small number can be interviewed and therefore only limited generalizations can be made, but it gives a deeper understanding of the issues. Secondly, the reliability and validity of the interview cannot be ascertained as in an attitude scale or even a questionnaire. However, to enhance its reliability and validity the researchers assured students that their responses will be treated strictly confidentially, and the use of a tape recorder was eschewed to remove any doubt from students' minds. Extensive notes were made during and after every session and then later on the same evening for analysis and interpretation. Tables 5.2 and 5.3 present students' responses.

Research Findings: Caste Awareness and Bullying

Three emerging themes will be addressed here: identity issues relating to caste consciousness and inter-caste relationship; emerging individualism; and scholastic achievement as interpreted by teachers. It is clear from Table 5.2 that the majority of students' parents are from a working-class background and that most mothers also work to supplement the family income.

Firstly we explore the views on caste amongst our respondents. A 14-year-old Chamar girl's response is interesting:

> I go to Guru Ravidas *gurdwara* regularly and also take part in services. I know he lived at the same time as Kabir in Benares near the river Ganges. I know a legend when he had disputed with Brahmins and won. Caste does exist but I do not believe in it. I think we are all equal.

> Some Jats and Brahmins think they are everything, but they are not. ... Jats drink a lot and fight and they say they are Sikhs but they are not. I have friends who are Jat girls and we follow Guru Nanak's teaching who was a follower of Guru Ravidas ji. Sikhs say he is a *bhagat* and not a *guru*. I have learnt all this from my Dad who is a *Sat Sangi* [devoted to Guru Ravidas ji]. I go back to my Punjabi village and we all celebrate *Lohri* (winter festival) where every one participates – Jats and all. Jats cannot say they are superior because Brahmin would say they are and so on.

A 12-year-old Jat girl gives a short answer as she is less concerned with the caste system:

> I want to be a doctor and I have a computer at home and my parents help me with homework. From here I'll go to a sixth form college to do 'A levels'. I have heard of Chamar and Jats, but I do not believe in it. We mix together. My Mum told me we are all Sikhs, so there should be no difference.

Another 15-year-old Chamar girl gave a very illuminating reply:

> My Mum works in a hospital and my dad is a teacher. At the end of the day
> you are all Punjabis. I think that Jat people think they are better – tease people
> not in school but outside school. I have no problem with that. In our school
> nothing like this – it may happen in another school. I consider myself as British-
> Asian. I am Chamar and I am learning to read and write Punjabi. I want to go
> to university and become a teacher. I am treated equally at home and we speak
> Punjabi and English at home.

A 15-year-old Jat boy comments:

> Sikhism is about equality. Caste teasing does happen but at a 'joke' level – it
> is not too serious. They should teach about caste in RE ... I do not think it will
> die, it will carry on. People won't let it go. I would marry in my own caste
> for two reasons. I do not want to upset my grandparents and in marriage you
> should be 100 per cent committed and it can only happen if your wife is from
> the same caste. Children learn it from their parents and so it goes on ... Some
> people look down on Chamars but my Dad thinks it is wrong to do so.

Another 15-year-old Jat boy:

> God is one, I believe, and you can go to any *gurdwara*. I do not notice any one's
> caste. Most of my friends are Chamars ... but when I get married it should be
> from the same caste. ... Bullying can happen but not in this school. Teachers
> do not mention it. You can teach it in RE, the history of caste and its bad side.
> [*Should there be a law to prohibit caste discrimination?*] Yes, there could be
> a law like race-relations.

Here we have a range of responses and only three out of 30 interviewees mentioned
caste teasing and bullying but qualified it to say it is not serious. But it is important
to note that they are all from the Chamar caste (20 per cent). They are all aware
of the Indian caste divisions and caste hierarchies as their parents talk to them
about it. Many students have overheard conversations of family friends and
relatives on caste-related matters. A repeated response on caste bullying was:
'It does not happen in our school – more as a joke.' This was repeated several
times by students, but this joke has a serious side to it. Allport (1954) notes that
racial jokes tend to reinforce stereotypes of ethnic minority groups and provide
a rationale for negative prejudice and discrimination. In India jokes about Sikhs
(were/are called *surds* – supposed to be a humorous abbreviation of *sardar*, that
is, chief) were told publically, even in polite society, and some Sikhs told them
themselves to gain favour from the majority Hindu community. In the UK 'Irish'
and 'Paki' jokes remained the staple diet of many stand-up comedians until the
Race Relations Act of 1971. Cynics dub this an era of 'politically correct' language

use. It is remarked that people should be able to enjoy jokes at the expense of disadvantaged, minority ethnic groups, and women. But, enlightened people think the opposite and say that ethnic and sexist jokes should be strongly disapproved of and condemned, especially in public.

Dhanda (2009) interviewed 24 Dalit young people in Wolverhampton, England, on caste awareness and caste bullying as part of a wider cross-national study on 'transitions in identity'. She writes: 'All those I interviewed reported experience of caste-related bullying in school, sometimes via exclusion, but mostly through name-calling ... their own early experience gets expressed in a reluctance to work in an all-Indian environment for fear of caste discrimination' (Dhanda, 2009: 57). The Anti Caste Discrimination Alliance (ACDA,[1] 2009 website) in a wide-ranging report on caste discrimination in the UK found evidence of caste bullying in schools. The majority of their respondents (77 per cent) in an online survey described their personal experience of caste-related insults and bullying. Eleven per cent had been subjected to physical abuse and threatening behaviour. A quotation from the report illustrates the point:

> My nephew, about five years ago, goes to ... school, basically got bullied at school. He came home and asked his dad about Chamars and Churas. Obviously some of the kids were taunting him because of his caste ... In the end we eventually moved to a different school ... We associate with *Ravidassia* ... low caste, whatever, but all the temples are based on caste discrimination... The proof is the number of gurdwaras we have by different communities ... (ACDA, 2009 website: 17).

We discussed the role of Sikh *gurdwaras* and other places of worship in perpetuating and reinforcing the caste system in Chapter 4. But briefly, despite the teaching of Sikh gurus on the equality of all human beings (irrespective of caste, gender, and class), Sikhs have not discontinued the Hindu practice of caste snobbery and discrimination (Puri, 2003). This has lead to serious divisions and rifts amongst Sikhs in the UK and elsewhere.

ACDA has successfully lobbied the House of Lords Committee to include caste in the Single Equality Bill. The Committee has acceded to the request provided that the Committee's commissioned large-scale research finds evidence of substantial caste discrimination in the delivery of public services (for detailed discussion see Chapter 4). Further rigorous studies are urgently needed to identify the special problems facing Dalit children and young people in schools and colleges.

---

1   ACDA stands for Anti Caste Discrimination Alliance which includes bodies such as CasteWatch UK and a Dalit national and international solidarity. A more rigorous Report by NIESR (Metcalf, H. and Rolfe, H. 2010) found evidence of 'caste' bullying.

Identity Issues

Who am I? To whom do I belong? Am I a Chamar, an Indian, a British person or do I possess some form of 'hyphenated' identity? These are some of the questions which are posed by many ethnic minority students (see Ghuman, 2003).

In the 1960s there was a stress on linear identity formation and closely associated with this was the notion that one partly inherits one's identity – a form of essentialism. You are born a Brahmin or a Jew and you stay that way. I am a Sikh or an Indian or British. Then in the 1970s emphasis shifted to bicultural and hyphenated identities, for example a British-Sikh or British-Asian and so on. Presently, a more nuanced approach has been adopted by researchers (Barrett, 2007) in the study of personal identities. This notion is conceptualized under the rubric of multiple identities, which advocates the importance of context within which personal identity is being described or ascribed. Thus a student may describe herself as an Indian when amongst a crowd of mixed ethnic background people. The same student, however, may describe herself as British when she is visiting relatives in India. And yet when she is mainly amongst male students she describes herself as a girl/woman. Thus the invocation of a particular type of identity would depend on the social context within which an individual is functioning and the significance one attaches to being a 'somebody' that would maintain and enhance one's self-esteem as a person. Hence the notion of fluid multiple identities has been advocated by scholars (Suarez-Orozco and Suarez-Orozco, 2001) who have studied minority ethnic students in multicultural contexts.

In the present study, however, students were asked a direct question on their identity, namely: What is your identity? Whom do you think you belong to? Students were prompted as in a multiple questionnaire: Indian, British, British-Indian, British-Asian, Sikh, Chamar, or any other.

From Table 5.3 we infer that most of the young people (19/30) described their identity in a hyphenated way. It was surprising to note that none of them described themselves as Asians – though a few identified as British Asians. The label Asian, which has been ascribed by indigenous white people (and the media) to include people of Pakistani and Bangladeshi origin seems to be replaced by 'Indian' etcetera. The main reason, in my view, is the rise of Indian economic power and prestige on the world stage on the one hand and the commensurate decline of Pakistan and Bangladesh on the other. The former is dubbed as a failed state and harbours terrorism and the latter as a poverty stricken and unstable country. Several high-caste people and Dalits in the interview told me that they are proud[2] to be Indian and declare themselves as such when on holiday or abroad. Whereas in the past it was an embarrassment to say Indian as 'we' were stereotyped as a poverty stricken and hungry nation which needed continuous help in feeding its starving millions.

---

2   I am not sure how the negative publicity (that is, corruption and inefficiency) over the 2010 Commonwealth Games in Delhi is going to affect their newly found pride.

No one identified oneself with being a Jat or Chamar. In other words they do not think primarily as belonging to a caste, which should be reassuring to people who believe young people are not as caste conscious as their forefathers/mothers were, and given time caste may be replaced by social class like in Britain and elsewhere in the West. A few representative responses go as follows: 'I am Indian/ British'; 'I think of myself as British/ Asian/Indian; I am a Sikh'; 'No I do not think my identity is Jat.' It would be interesting to undertake a cross-sectional study, with age and sex as two variables, to find out when/ or if caste becomes a salient feature of personal identity.

General Discussion with Sixth Form Students on Caste

The atmosphere in the discussion was relaxed and (18) students spoke their minds. There was no tension within the group. It became obvious to the writer from their conversation that they were dating and mixing freely and it was an accepted part of life. The teachers told me how the students use text messages and cell phones to arrange meetings and many parents now turn a blind eye.

The discussion was dominated by two students – a Chamar and a Ghumar (potter caste). Music was mentioned as one of the factors promoting or retarding integration of communities. 'Jat discs' are banned in the Punjab (someone said) because they glorify 'Jatism' – superiority of Jats. I was not able to verify this statement. But an article in *The Times* (5 July, 2010) by Kennedy seems to endorse that young Jat people are asserting their dominance in Britain:

> The Jat identity – the agricultural caste from Punjab whose musical traditions have derived from harvest celebrations – is promoted through bhangra music. Countless artists use Jat in their names and the word is frequently heard in song lyrics … the Jat character in these lyrics tend to be proud, lovable rogues and sometimes heavy drinkers … the debut single Jat Punjabi by Y-Vern beats was an instant hit.

A consensus emerged amongst the students that teaching of caste history could be a good idea as it will broaden their understanding. When I asked how many can read and write Punjabi, only two out of 30 students responded positively. There are no caste differences in achievement, according to the students.[3] None of the students has heard of Mangoo Ram or Dr Ambedkar – the two eminent leaders of the Dalit movement. On the future of the caste system, opinions varied from being very optimistic that caste would disappear, to pessimistic that it will endure for a very long time because it is so ingrained in the Indian psyche. Girls participated equally in the discussion and they were not inhibited and expressed their views freely. The students were of the opinion that the great leveller of caste differences

---

3   This is confirmed by teachers – see next chapter.

is the financial situation of the family. Half of the students' mothers were born in this country and were very open-minded about caste and wanted their children to be happy whoever they marry, that is, irrespective of caste and race. Almost all of the interviewees have been to India and enjoyed their stay. They met their extended families and felt at home, but they were not willing to live there except two boys who were studying IT and felt it offers them greater opportunities. They would like to work in the UK and save money and then settle in India. None of the girls wanted to live in India as they enjoyed their freedom in this country. Some girls thought boys enjoy more freedom and had to do fewer chores and are favoured generally. All of them wanted to go to a university and follow a profession. Most of them mentioned 'old universities' and wanted to study science or IT subjects.

Gender Differences

It is interesting to note that half (15/30 Table 5.3) the students think that boys and girls are treated equally at home, in relation to such things as pocket money, allocation of household chores, being allowed to go out with friends. The other half – mostly girls – think that boys still get preferential treatment, especially in being allowed to go out with friends. However, two boys remarked that their sisters are favoured in all sorts of ways by their mothers, and even spoilt. However, as for as school education and higher education is concerned, most of the sample said that they are given equal opportunity. In the next chapter the reader will learn that Dalit parents are keen to see their daughters enjoy the same educational facilities as their sons. This is in sharp contrast to the views of the first-generation who thought the education of boys should take precedence over girls, as the former are expected to support their elderly parents (see Ghuman, 1975). It seems that parents who are born here have fully acculturated into the norms of British society, on this respect at least. However, we need further research with large samples to validate this trend.

Educational Matters

We now turn to educational matters on which students' opinion were sought. As regards languages spoken at home, half the sample speaks only English and none speaks Punjabi, but others admit to using both depending on the context. For instance, with grandparents many students speak Punjabi but switch to English when speaking to their parents and siblings. Only two students are learning to read and write Punjabi. Most parents and students think that Punjabi (Hindi) is fine at a spoken level but that they should not spend any more time and effort in learning the language of their forefathers/mothers. This is partly justified[4] in an

---

4   Perhaps they have heard this from their teachers and parents.

outdated theory in which the mind is compared to a 'balloon' (Baker, 1995). As the analogy suggests, there is a limited capacity in the brain to learn and master facts, concepts, and languages, therefore one should deploy it to master what is going to be the most useful in one's life, *ergo* vocational aspect of education. Such a view has been challenged by psychologists (Baker, 1995; Bellin, 1995; Surez-Orozco and Surez-Orozco, 2001). Ports and Rumbaut (2001: 134) conclude from their longitudinal study of 14,000 second-generation young people in the US: 'Data shows a clear pattern where fluency in two languages is associated with benign social and psychological outcomes.'

Contemporary thinking on bilingualism therefore suggests that school curricula should offer a wide range of subjects and students should be encouraged to study as many languages as they would like. However, there are many practical difficulties in teaching community languages in schools. These have been discussed by the author elsewhere (Ghuman, 2003) and other by scholars (Bhatti, 1999; Baker, 1995). Briefly, these relate to a lack of material resources and qualified teachers, and time-tabling difficulties. In some cases even parents want to be pragmatic and want their children to concentrate on maths, science, and IT subjects as is also clear form our small sample (The reader's attention is directed to Chapter 4 where the role of *gurdwaras* in the teaching of Punjabi is discussed).

According to the interviewees, their parents are educationally orientated and want them to be qualified persons who can obtain lucrative jobs. All of them said they have access to computers and there is someone (Mum, Dad, older sibling) in the house to help them with their homework. Some parents arrange for extra tuition to help them achieve good grades.

As noted earlier in this chapter, many of them have visited India with their parents and enjoyed their stay. But all of them want to live in the UK, except two students who want to pursue a career and eventually settle in India. The following quotation sums up their attitude:

> It is lovely to see so many Indian famous buildings and meet one's relatives but the traffic noise and chaos is overwhelming. It is also very dirty and so much poverty, and corruption … It is very upsetting.

Acculturation/Enculturation

Acculturation may be defined as the process by which immigrants adapt to the ways of life of their host society. One researcher (Weinreich, 2009) refers to this process as a 'two-way' process and calls it enculturation, unlike acculturation where adaptation is unidirectional and in favour of a majority culture. Berry and Sabatier (2009) has developed an elaborate model of acculturation which outlines four strategies of acculturation, namely integration, separation, assimilation, and marginalization. Critics (Rudimen, 2003; Chirkov, 2009; Weinreich, 2009) maintain that this is an over simplified perspective on a very complex social adaptation process and have suggested a more nuanced approach to research. Detailed discussion of this topic is not relevant to the major theme of this book but the interested reader can follow the debate in the special issue of *International Journal of Intercultural Relations* edited by Chirkov (2009).

To study the acculturation of Indian/Asian young people the author (Ghuman, 2000, 2003) has constructed a scale and used it with young people in Australia, Canada, England, and the US. I found that Indian young people (mostly Hindus and Sikhs[5]) prefer to integrate with British society's norms as far as gender equality, secularism, and individualistic mode of living are concerned. They reject traditional gender inequality, dominance of religion, and collective and a familial way of living. Not surprisingly, girls in the study were found to be more highly in favour of acculturating to European/American norms than boys. Though no objective measures were used in this research to study this topic, we have enough data to throw some light on the process. Young people interviewed for this study are using their newly acquired skills to arrange dating, going out, and engaging in leisure activities. Girls are as confident as boys showing 'equality' with boys in the availability of educational facilities, but have not achieved parity in the spheres of social activities. Their vocational and professional expectations are similar to boys and they are not going to be married off at 16. Students' preferred/first language is English and their hopes and aspirations are similar to their British counterparts. Their mode of dress, the food they eat, TV they watch, and leisure activities are close to their white British peers. From all these indices we draw the conclusion that like other Indian young people previously studied (Ghuman, 2000, 2003), they are integrating with multicultural British society in a positive way. They still retain some elements of Indian culture, namely, knowledge of spoken Punjabi, deep respect for their parents, elements of their family religion, and attachment to India. They are happy at their multicultural schools, enjoy the school curricula, and nurture high vocational aspirations.

The findings of this chapter are encouraging to parents who are deeply interested in their children's education and welfare. The following chapter explores the views of parents and teachers on a variety of issues discussed in this chapter and forges links between the contents of these two chapters.

---

5   Hindus and Sikhs score higher on the acculturation scale than Muslim young people. The latter were found to be more traditional, preferring their community's lifestyle (Ghuman, 2003: 123–5).

Chapter 6
Teachers' and Parents' Views on Caste and Educational Matters

> I say invest in children's education. It is the best thing our community can do.
> I was a graduate when I came to this country but had to work as a labourer in a
> factory … Education is the main way to achieve social mobility and claim our
> rights. (Dalit Grandfather)

One of the chief motives for the emigration of Indian parents to Western countries
was to make use of the educational opportunities offered by the country of
adoption (Ghuman, 1999). Most of the emigrants belonged to the middle class of
Indian society and consequently nurtured high aspirations for their children. These
aspirations were built on the role models offered them by the elites of India. It is
a common practice amongst the elite to educate their children in English-medium
schools and then to send them abroad, especially to Britain and the US, for higher
education.

Successful education depends upon teachers who give unequivocal support to
their charges and are fully committed to their welfare. Their attitudes and views
are likely to be emulated by their students and are bound to affect their life styles
and chances. Parents who are equal partners in their children's education need
to understand how the school system works and what they can actively do to
support their children and exploit the educational facilities to the full. In the case
of minority ethnic groups there is an additional problem of cultural conflict arising
out of differences in attitudes and values between home and school[1] (Ghuman,
1980, 1994). There is a real risk that cultural discontinuity between ethnic minority
homes and school may impede the educational progress of students. We conducted
semi-structured interviews with a number of teachers and parents. These are based
on the topics presented in Appendix B (135–6). Table 6.1 presents the details of
the samples.

The teachers and head teachers were interviewed from the two schools from
where we took the sample of students described in the last chapter. Of the 24
parents interviewed, half of them had children at the two schools selected for the
study. The 12 other parents' children were also studying in secondary schools and
colleges of higher education.

Parents' interviews were conducted bilingually at their homes, whereas teachers
and governors were interviewed in English at school venues. A tape recorder was

---

1 Of course there are many aspects of schooling on which parents and teachers fully
agree, namely, high achievement, discipline, good manners, and respect for seniors.

Table 6.1   Details of teachers, parents, and others interviewed

Professionals/ parents	Males	Females	
Teachers	4	4	8
Head teachers	2	–	2
Dalit parents	10	6	16
High-caste parents	5	3	8
Total	**21**	**13**	**34**

used in four interviews and then discarded in favour of taking extensive notes both during and after the interviews. The chief reason in favour of notes was that respondents felt rather inhibited and became self-conscious when the tape-recorder was switched on, despite my assurance that all the material collected would be highly confidential. Tape-recorder malfunctions were also disruptive.

Teachers' Views on Caste

We are going to quote extensively from our interviews to give readers both the content and flavour of interviewees' perceptions and attitudes on caste and educational matters.

A Dalit woman teacher with six years' teaching experience commented:

Caste does not cause any problems in this school. Most children are vaguely aware of its existence but it does not bother them. My own son is aware of it but we do not make a big thing out of it. In India, it is very different … My family is politically very active and so was I, but here I concentrate on my family and my teaching. I was a neighbour of Kanshi Ram and we lived closed to Mangoo Ram [both eminent Dalit leaders]. He used to come to our house and hold me in his lap ... There are no behaviour problems at school and girls have not complained about it. We have had nothing as regards caste from parents. I did not experience any caste-related queries when I was at university.

However, a Dalit governor of a school had a different point of view:

I did not face any problem at school – that is some 25 years ago, but in college, yes. They asked me which *gurdwara* I go to and what is my surname? And so on. Then I asked my father what it is about caste that I am being questioned. Then I had a conflict with my own people as it were because they did not tell me about it. This is in 1978.

There is a bad feeling in the community right now [June, 2009] because of the murder of Sant Ramanand. I have met him and had his blessings. He was like my personal guru and a very gentle person. There is a lot about this on the YouTube and this is a burning issue. I rang up my cousin in Jalandhar (Punjab) and they said we have riots here – we have to do this to make our feelings known and make a statement that we do matter. We can also be *saheed* [martyrs] and sacrifice in the name of our quom like Jats and others.

A Ramgarhia Sikh (male) teacher and president of his community's *gurdwara* had a very different angle:

Girls from Chamar families have an inferiority complex and they think that I am going to look down upon them, but this is not the case. Actually, *gurdwaras* were originally set up by our community, but they were taken over by Jats. They are quarrelsome people so we have to establish our own to avoid petty squabbling … Ravidas *bhavans* are like *gurdwaras* but they do not want to be associated with us. They want to maintain their independence … Yes, they do follow the same type of services as us but they stress the importance of Guru Ravidas whom we treat as a saint – *bhagat*. They do not want to be called 'Raidas' Sikhs but the follower of Guru Ravidas … Chamars are putting up barriers themselves and then they blame us for treating them badly. They have that sort of complex. In India, in a way there is more mixing. Four of my friends were Chamars and only one from my own caste, and all of them are teachers.

There are some high-caste teachers and parents who are sympathetic to such a style of argument. This was described in Chapter 4 of the book. Such an interpretation can also be seen as blaming the victims of their own inferior economic conditions and social status. People of high status invoke explanations such as: 'They have a chip on their shoulders'; 'Why don't they pull themselves up by their bootstraps rather than complaining?'

A deputy head teacher (male) from a high caste says:

I have been in the school for 19 years and have never come across this issue. But that is not to say it is not discussed amongst students. I am sure they know and talk about it, but it has never been a significant problem. [*Should there be a law like race-relations*?] No, there is no need for a law as it is a personal thing. Look H … [Dalit governor] and I have known each other for a good 20 years but have never talked about caste. (My italics)

I was surprised to hear from a senior experienced teacher that caste is purely a personal matter and not a social one. A similar comment was made at a CasteWatch Conference (May 2009) by a high-caste county councillor. He argued people should not 'whinge and moan about it but rise above it'. I am reminded of these types of arguments which were put forward by many well-meaning teachers who opposed the inclusion of anti-racist elements in the school curricula.

A female governor (caste not known) commented:

> I teach in a majority Asian school and never have come across complaints on this issue. But there are other areas of conflict – religion. For instance, why do people of particular religion have more holidays? It is about time the Indian community should move on and focus on issues, which their kids really face in schools.

Thus, we have a range of responses from our teachers and governors. Overall, from this small group it emerges that 'caste' is not a significant problem in these two schools. Furthermore, the teachers in the study think that it cannot be equated with race issues. Their comments are revealing. A deputy head remarked:

> This is not a salient issue and I do not think it merits the same treatment as racism. This topic is not covered in the syllabus, but it is a sensitive issue in the school. There have been minor incidents but we never had any complaints from the parents.

A Headmaster commented:

> The majority of teachers do not know in any detail about the caste system. Indian teachers surely know and are well aware of it, but I do not think it is a significant issue which needs addressing. Certainly it is not considered on par with racism. The Ravidas community has bought the old building adjacent to our school and intend to use it as a community and educational centre, but it has no impact on our school … I do not think a law is necessary it would be counterproductive to equal opportunity. It will do more harm than good. The staff is aware of it and it surfaces from time to time, but parents have not come to school to say this is an issue, which need addressing. In our sixth form we have mostly Muslim girls the reasons for which you understand is that Sikh and other Asians go to colleges of further education as they like freedom, and choice … We do not have any problems at our school of a religious nature either.

Teachers were asked, if we were to teach about the Hindu caste system, which subject(s) in the school curricula is/are suitable. We had an interesting range of replies. A woman teacher gave a thoughtful answer:

> This topic is not covered in the syllabus, but it is a sensitive issue in the school … May be it can be included in Religious Education. There have been minor incidents but we never had any complaints from the parents. If it does happen, it is between Chamar and Jat families. It is mostly with the older generation but young people are not bothered with this topic. There are a few inter-caste

marriages in the two communities but they are not that common. As regards law,
I doubt if it could be given a practical shape and the issue would be blown out
of all proportion.

An academic I interviewed for this research had a similar ambivalent view of
legislating against caste discrimination and thereby giving it so much publicity.
According to her, many people from her Chamar community in the UK even
object to being called Dalits (oppressed people), as the host community does not
make any distinction when dealing with Indians.

Although, casteism cannot be strictly equated with racism in terms of its
spread and the pain it inflicts, some of the arguments which teachers use to exclude
it from the school curricula are similar to the ones that put forward when the
implementation of anti-racist education was advocated. In my view, as discussed
in the last chapter, caste issues can be included in history and RE (Religious
Education) lessons and should strengthen the multicultural perspective of the
school curricula.

School Achievement

The academic performance of students is linked to a host of sociological and
psychological factors. There have been literally hundreds of studies on this issue.
However, for the purpose of this book the reader is referred to Vernon's books
(1969, 1982) which comprehensively deal with the impact of socio-cultural
factors on school achievement. Research on ethnicity and school performance
is also extensive both in the UK and USA, and rates the performance of Indian
students 'highly' – just below the Chinese-origin students but higher than other
ethnic groups.[2] This success is explained by the cultural-ecological theory of Ogbu
(1995) who conducted a number of studies on minority ethnic groups in the US.
The key element of his theory postulates that important factors in high achievement
are positive attitudes of minority ethnic parents towards their society of adoption,
high expectations of parents of their children, and encouragement and support
students receive to learn English. In his view, children of such ethnic communities
internalize these positive values and attitudes and outperform their peers.

A number of research studies in the UK (Gillborn and Gipps, 1996; Gillborn
and Mirza, 2000; Ghuman, 2003) have clearly established that Indian students
outperform their white and black peers but are below the Chinese-origin students
in the GCSE examination (General Certificate of Secondary Education). This
confirms Ogbu's theory of school achievement outlined above. It is also important
to mention, albeit briefly, the insights of Suarez-Orozco and Suarez-Orozco (2001)
in this context, who have researched extensively on the achievement of minority

---

2   For details of research in the US see Ogbu (1994, 1995) and Ports and Rumbout
(2001). For UK studies see the DFES website (2005), accessed 10 October, 2010.

ethnic students in the US. They argue that those young people who counteract racial prejudice and negative stereotyping though retaining hope for the future and thereby preserve their self-esteem and pride are the ones who advance, whereas those who become hopeless and nurture self-doubt tend to lose out. In sum, success in school examinations is chiefly a motivational problem and is not linked to inherited cognitive abilities.

Of course, Indian students hail from a variety of caste and religious backgrounds, and statistics on a caste basis are not available. Therefore, we asked all the interviewees a crucial question on academic performance, viz.: Is there any significant difference between Dalit boys and girls and their Indian peers of high caste? The response of all the interviewees was a definite 'no'. Their judgement was based on their extensive professional experience. Likewise, high-caste parents, with the exception of a few, believe that there is no difference between Dalit and high-caste children and young people. However, one of the male teachers made the following observation:

> Academic performance of Indian students has dipped somewhat because they have now developed other interests outside academia. Parents have less control over their children and in some cases, parents are afraid of their children because so many agencies champion their cause and they are fluent English speakers ... I know some of them intimidate their parents.

Two other teachers agreed with this observation. This may be owing to their wider interests (including dating and going out) and lower motivation to achieve academic success. A similar situation prevailed in Yuba City, California (Ghuman, 2003), where a teacher remarked:

> A third generation is different from 'fresh off the boat' students who worked hard for their grades and showed respect to teachers. These kids have caught the 'negative' attitudes of American students and 'boys have discovered girls', and 'girls have found boys' and their academic performance is falling. Now I see them cuddling and caressing around the play yard like the white kids.

Zhang Z. (2009), researching Chinese-origin young people, found a similar trend in Vancouver, Canada. It makes sense when one reflects upon the predicament of young people in multicultural settings. They are bound to be influenced by the youth culture prevailing in Western countries where dating, outings, and drinking are the norms (admittedly, there are class and family differences) and school work is not considered to be the 'be all and end all' (Gibson, 1988). In developing countries like India and China there is enormous pressure on students to excel in examinations as the competition for entry into prestigious universities is very stiff indeed. Marks over 80 per cent are required to become eligible for admission to science, engineering, IT, and medicine courses. It follows that in the 'first-generation' Indian and Chinese students 'motivation to achieve' is extremely high and students work hard to excel in academic subjects. The second-and subsequent generations tend to acculturate and lose their strong drive to achieve.

Indian boys and girls tend to play together as do other ethnic groups observed an experienced teacher:

> Indian boys and girls tend to stick together as do the other ethnic groups, but to my knowledge, segregation or grouping on account of caste does not take place. It is possible that this happens when students are older and parents put pressure on them to seek friendship from within their own caste with a view to getting married.

To summarize, none of the teachers mentioned any difference in achievement or behaviour of Dalit boys and girls compared to their Indian peers. Girls are given equal opportunity with boys as far as education is concerned, according to the teachers in the study. This is in sharp contrast to first-generation Indian immigrants whose boys tended to receive preferential treatment compared to girls (Ghuman, 1975).

Parents' Interviews

The aims of interviewing a sample of parents were twofold: to discover their attitude to the British education system, and to assess their views on caste awareness of their young people. All the parents I interviewed, except a single parent family, were highly motivated to help their children to secure the best education the English system can offer. They have followed the advice of their inspiring leader, Baba Sahib Ambedkar, whose clarion call to Dalits was: 'organize, educate, and agitate'. The community is well organized and can always mobilize support for its causes through their *bhavans* and Buddhist temples. Many followers of Dr Ambedkar have converted to Buddhism. Above all, they consider education a means of social mobility. A Dalit grandfather, whose two sons gained degrees from Oxford and Cambridge and now can count nine members of his family holding postgraduate degrees, made a telling observation:

> I say invest in children's education. It is the best thing our community can do. My family spends over forty thousand pounds on the private education of grandchildren ... I was a graduate when I came to this country but had to work as a labourer in a factory ... I was determined to give the very best opportunities to my children. Education is the main way to achieve social mobility and claim our rights.

He proudly showed me pictures of his sons in degree ceremonies in their academic gowns. On this perspective, he was not alone, a taxi driver said:

I told my son and daughter when they were in grammar school, if you need tuition in any subjects let me know, but they declined. My daughter has completed her degree and my son is at a university. I am very pleased with their education. I do not make any distinction between my boy and girl – both deserve the best.

A retired businessman was very glad that he had emigrated to England and had his children educated in this country. He commented:

My son is a qualified graduate teacher, who now runs his own private academy to coach students for 11+ examination [selection tests are still held in some LEAS]. Indian parents are very keen that their children should be selected for grammar school education as they think it is better than their counterpart comprehensive schools. They think education should help them to move up the economic and social ladder.

A high-caste father was of the opinion that Dalit young people are going to university just like their counterparts from other Indian communities. He was of the view that Chamars and Valmikis are financially as successful as high-caste communities are because they do not face any caste discrimination from the indigenous whites in this country; and they are hard-working people.

However, one high-caste father was very cynical in his views:

Dalit and Singh [meaning Sikhs who wear beards and turbans] people do not know how to behave properly on parents' days and talk to teachers. Their children leave school at 16 and then drift into drugs and alcoholism ... then they blame others for their failures. Also, they condemn Hindu gods out of spite and say they are Buddhist, and the joke is that they do not know anything about it. They should know that Gautama Buddha was a high-caste Hindu. Likewise Sikh gurus were all from my religion and their basic beliefs are derived from us, but they think they are a separate quom.

This was the only dissenting voice I heard from my interviewees on the educational achievement and aspiration of Dalits. He was generally disparaging of Dalit communities (and the Sikh community) and their achievements both in the UK and in India. This was discussed in Chapter 4 of the book. Briefly, the psychological explanation is given by scholars, following Allport's theory of prejudice (Dovidio et al., 2005: 5): 'Insecurity, fear, and anxiety can stimulate a need for self-enhancement, which in some cases creates or exacerbates prejudice.' Many Indians in the UK, irrespective of caste, face racial prejudice and discrimination[3] in all walks of life and this threatens their traditional status. Thus they tend to disparage their countrymen to compensate for the loss of their social status. Allport's (1954)

---

3   Many people in Britain refer to all South Asians as Pakis or still use the word coloured to include people from the West Indies.

original thesis was that fundamental motives for group prejudice are to maintain power, status, and control to meet one's ideals and aspirations.

A single-mother who lives in a council house had this to say:

> My son is in the third form [14-years-old] and daughter has already left school at 16 and now works as a sales girl. I cannot help them as much as I would like to because I have to work and manage the house and look after my elderly parents. Their father does not bother to help them … I know education is a good thing and we should have as much as we can.

Dalit Parents and Caste Issues

Nearly half the Dalit parents expressed the view that schools should address caste issues in the school curriculum. Their reasoning is based on the belief that children have to face caste-related problems when they grow up. They argue that it is a social problem for the Indian-origin students. A Dalit woman parent (and a teacher, age 40+) observed:

> A balanced history of the caste system should be taught in either religious classes or social studies … To this end new books should be written as the traditional interpretations tend to justify caste on spurious grounds [Here she refers to a Hindu Council Report – 2008 – see my comments on the Report in Chapter 2 (26–8)] … When I was at school 25 years ago, Indian people were all united because the number was small. Now we have grown in size and caste divisions have come into play again.

Those schools which have a small intake of Indian students do not bother about caste, but in a majority Asian school students tend to experience divisions along caste lines. However, the reader should note that in the two schools[4] studied in this research caste was not considered a problem by teachers and parents.

A community leader (age 45+) who is active in a Dalit movement has this to say on the issue:

> The situation is such that both the victims and the oppressors do not wish to acknowledge that the caste system is alive and kicking in the UK. This is a curious psychological phenomenon. In my view, the victims hide their identity to enhance their self-respect in a dubious way and the oppressors feel guilty that they are perpetuating caste divisions in this day and age … In schools it should be possible to study caste issues objectively so that it does not become a psychological problem for youngsters later in life.

---

4   Both schools are in neighbourhood with a high of concentration of South Asians.

This is a substantial point and needs further clarification and discussion. Allport's theory (1954: Chapter 20) on prejudice and its subsequent development by Devine (2005) explains the position of an oppressor. He/she does not acknowledge his/ her prejudice owing to the inner conflict of competing loyalties to one's tradition (and religion in the case of Hindus) on the one hand, and the democratic notion of equality and dignity of all citizens on the other. This type of inner conflict can lead to the experience of 'prejudice with compunction' (that is, accompanied by shame, guilt, and regret). Therefore it is quite likely that people in this situation would avoid facing their caste prejudice; and if they did, they would try to rationalize it. As regards victims of prejudice, 'denial' is simply a form of escapism to maintain one's self esteem and human dignity. Findings from the Social Identity Theory (Tajfel, H., 1982)[5] suggests positive measures which victims of discrimination may pursue, namely, individual mobility and social competition with out-groups. In Britain Dalits have been as successful, if not more, than their high-caste peers, thus enhancing their self-esteem and group solidarity, and they may not want to lower their self-image by admitting that they belonged to an Untouchable caste.

Another point of view is that many Indians of all castes want to minimize traditional caste divisions (except when it comes to marriage) in the hope that in a generation or two it will wither away. A Jat mother (age 50+), who has a son and a daughter, observed:

> One of my friends is a 'Churi' (Valmiki) and I do not mind it at all. They are Gills ... Somebody told me this and I said it does not matter. They have a nice house, and both husband and wife work ... She wants to keep quiet about it. Most parents would prefer that their children marry within their own caste but they have to accept inter-caste and inter-racial marriages ... I would say 80 per cent of people do not know about caste in this country and they learn about it when they go to India!

A Jat professional (age 50+), his brother, and wife gave some very reflective answers:

> In our village (in India) they have not made much progress. They are still doing menial jobs and few have become teachers or nurses but no one has achieved a higher professional status – like a doctor ... In this country I do not know any Dalits. I think most of them would hide their identity to save any come back ... The caste system is abhorrent as it violates the basic human rights ... My sons

---

5   This theory is formulated from extensive empirical research with social groups. Simply put, it states that there appears to be a need for every social group to create and maintain positively-valued social identity, and this is achieved by comparison to out-group or groups who are often characterized negatively. The membership of a group may be based on criteria of race, caste or class (Ghuman, 1999: 44).

do not know anything about caste … In India the caste system would endure for centuries.

His wife says she would prefer her sons to find girls from within her own caste but she may not be consulted: 'My sons are very independent and I may not have a say … I am 80 per cent against and 20 per cent in favour.' Her brother says: 'I would not go that far because of the pressure of tradition of the Indian community.'

Concluding Remarks

From the comments of parents and community leaders and my observations at Dalit temples, community centres, and homes it became clear that Dalit students are achieving 'good' examination grades as are their counterparts from other Indian communities. Dalit parents are very pleased with the British system of education and have fully availed themselves of the facilities offered. According to my assessment, their young people are entering universities and higher institutions of learning at the same rate as their counterparts from other Indian communities.

Most parents I have interviewed would prefer their young people to marry within their own caste and religion. However, they are also beginning to consider the feelings and sentiments of their young people as many have seen failed arranged marriages, especially when one of the partners is from India. This shift to a degree also reflects their changing attitude from a collective to an individual mode of seeing the world. People with a collective orientation view the world from the familial, kinship, and societal perspective whereas the individualists see the world from their own perspective and say: 'what do I get out of this' rather than 'what do we get out of it'. A wider discussion on this topic is to be found in my previous writing (Ghuman, 1999).

Girls are becoming more confident and demanding equality with boys, and are availing themselves of the full opportunities offered by the British system of education. Girls of Indian origin are outperforming boys in school examinations and obtaining good jobs. There is no doubt in my mind that Dalit girls are as good as their Indian and white peers. All this can be attributed to Dalit parents' high aspirations for their girls, teachers' dedication and hard work, and the determination and motivation of the girls.

Chapter 7
Reflections and Application

We set out to explore the concerns and issues facing Indian Dalit communities in the English Midlands and on this quest we have been amply rewarded. A cautionary note is important here. The main findings of the research strictly relate to this locale and population; however its results should have relevance to Dalit communities in the UK and beyond. Indeed, the research should throw light on Dalits from Pakistan, Bangladesh, and Nepal. The book has pursued three inter-related themes: the reproduction of caste awareness and divisions amongst Indian immigrants[1] in the UK; the role of religion and other agencies in perpetuating caste consciousness; the role of education and Dalit-lead initiatives in counteracting the negative affects of caste prejudice and discrimination.

In the 1960s and mid-1970s there was little caste awareness among Indian immigrants. They were mostly male workers who shared rooms, houses and attended newly founded places of worship such as *gurdwaras*. In the next two decades, the number of Indians dramatically increased owing to two salient factors: further emigration from India and East Africa, and single men were joined by their families and sponsored relatives.

Places of Religious Worship

According to our interviewees, acute caste awareness began in the late 1970s in Indian enclaves such as Handsworth, Birmingham, and Southhall, London. High caste people began to ask questions about 'caste' such as: which village do you come from? What is your surname? The chief purpose of such questioning was to exclude people of lower castes from social and religious intercourse. No doubt, some high-caste people thought they would gain power and advantage over their low-caste and outcaste countrymen. This happened mainly in *gurdwaras* which ironically are supposed to be caste levellers, according to the teaching of Sikh gurus. Dalit persons who were fully baptized Sikhs were discriminated and not allowed to distribute *prasad* to the *sangat* (congregation), and join the management team of *gurdwaras*. Likewise Hindu priests in *mandirs* began to question the rights of Dalits to perform *puja* ceremonies. This galvanized the two major Dalit communities of Chamars and Valmikis in the UK to raise funds and build their own *bhavans* and temples respectively. The rise of educated second-generation Dalits also contributed to the widening fissure amongst the Indian community.

---

1   Many of them are now second and third generation citizens of the UK.

They were not willing to put up with the arrogant and prejudiced attitudes of high-caste people and to be excluded from places of worship. Most of them were born in the UK and did not want to hide their caste identities, but instead took pride in them. I was repeatedly told by both young people and parents: 'I am proud to be a Chamar/ Valmiki. I am as good as Jats'[2] (Dhanda, 2009). From this time on (circa 1975s), Indians increasingly began to socialize separately, such as visiting caste and family friends and relatives at weekends. It was quite common for Punjabi factory workers to patronize different pubs in Birmingham and Coventry and fights broke out frequently between Jats and Valmikis.

Sikh *gurdwaras* in the UK, North America and Europe are now established along caste lines and are reproducing and reinforcing cast divisions amongst their devotees. Ravidasi communities call their places of worship *bhavans* rather than *gurdwaras* for the reasons explained in Chapter 4 of this book. Briefly, they do not wish to come under the jurisdiction of the Shri Gurdwara Parbandhank Committee (SGPC) in Amritsar, Punjab, and lose their freedom to manage and control their *bhavans*. However, readers should note that modes of worship and religious services in *bhavans* are virtually the same as those in *gurdwaras* with one notable exception. In some *bhavans*, they allow visiting Indian saints to claim equal status to the *Guru Granth Sahib*, the holy book of the Sikhs.[3] These saints seat themselves on the same podium as the holy book or at a similar dais and expect the *sangat* (congregation) to prostrate themselves before them. They also allow them to raise funds for charitable causes (some say for dubious causes; Case Study 6) in India and are not accountable to the local management committee. This has caused deep division and friction between Chamar and Jat Sikh communities in both the UK and India. A recent event in which Shri Ramanand was murdered in a *bhavan* in Austria (allegedly by Sikh fundamentalists) has sparked off a huge protest in the UK and riots in north India. Several people died during these riots.

The above described historical and contemporary events have coalesced and led the followers of Guru Ravidas to announce (*Sunday Times of India*, 31 January, 2010) their intention to revive the pledge of Mangoo Ram (see Chapter 2) and build on the teaching of their guru and initiate a new religion in his name with their own holy book, emblems, and liturgy. This is being hotly discussed on the TV and elsewhere in the Punjab,[4] as the SGPC is concerned with the potential permanent fissure within Sikh communities. The SGPC's perspective is that the *Adi Granth*

---

2   However some people and associations, for example, ACDA (2009), may disagree with this comment. They feel Chamar is a derogatory and insulting name given by high-caste people. Certainly Valmikis, when they are referred to as Churas (sweepers and cleaners), feel humiliated and find the word most offensive – akin to the word 'nigger' used by whites in the US to describe/address African-Americans.

3   In the final *ardas* (prayer), rather than following strict Sikh tradition of: '*Jo bhole so nihal; sat siri akal*', they say '*jo bhole so nirbah* (fearless), *Siri Guru Ravidas ki jai.*' (*Sangat* in *bhavans* glorifies Guru Ravidas rather than 'God is truth' of the traditional Sikh prayer).

4   See the note at the end of the chapter.

– the holy book of the Sikhs – does embrace the hymns of Guru Ravidas, and that he is widely respected amongst all Sikhs and they should remain united. Furthermore, they contend that the teaching of Sikh gurus forbids caste and gender discrimination and that Sikhs have instituted the *langar* (community kitchen) and *pangat* (eat together on the mats, see Chapter 2) to get rid of untouchability. The argument runs that this proposed new religion would appeal only to the Chamar community and there would be other outcaste people such as Valmikis who would still be left outside the fold, therefore the main objective of the proposed religion would not be realized.[5]

The Valmiki community has built its own places of worship and is proud to be independent of both Hindu temples and Sikh *gurdwaras*. Although their holy book is the *Ramayana* of Hindus, their services are mixtures of Sikh and Hindu modes of worship (Nesbitt, 1991). Some Valmikis have converted to Christianity and this practice of conversion goes back to the 1920s (Juergensmeyer, 1982). Furthermore, some Valmikis have continued to practise Sikhism to which their forefathers/mothers converted since the establishment of *Khalsa* by the tenth guru, Guru Gobind Singh. They are called Mazhabi Singhs and were an important part of the British Raj army and this tradition continues to this day.

In sum, paradoxically the places of religious worship have created fissures amongst Indian communities rather than uniting them to fight for racial equality and fair play in the UK and elsewhere. However, they have bestowed immense social and political status on the Dalit communities. At an individual level people feel proud of their caste affiliations and are mobilizing support for their rights in the UK, India, North America, and Europe.

Inter-caste Marriages

There is no doubting the fact that the institutions of family and marriage are the bastion of caste retention and divisions. There is a vast amount of research (Ballard, 1994; Stopes-Roe and Cochrane, 1990; Ghuman, 1994; Shaw, 2000) which affirms that most marriages in the first- and -second-generation Indians are arranged along caste and religious lines. These were/are accomplished through established channels of kith and kin, ads in English-medium and vernacular papers, and special marriage bureaus which sprang up to fill this need of the Indian communities in the UK and elsewhere. Currently electronic media is increasingly used to facilitate unions. Due to endogamy caste divisions are now alive and well and caste consciousness is further strengthened by the religious institutions as we have discussed above. One of the aims of the research was to find out parents' and young people's views on inter-caste marriages. Both high-caste and Dalit parents

---

5   There is also deep division within Ravidasis on this issue. One of the sections wants to keep the status quo whilst the other wants to split from the mainstream Sikh religion (ACDA, 2009; Singh and Tatla, 2006).

in the interviews were of the opinion that the custom of within-caste marriage is bound to continue for another generation or so, but a few conceded that they will be powerless to stop their young people choosing partners from another caste, race, or religion. Their opinions were based on familiar grounds: 'What would their *biraderi* and kinship say?' They also pointed out the difficulties which many inter-caste couples have faced in both the UK and India (Dhanda, 2009; Ghuman, 2003). A personalized account is written by a Jat woman (Sanghera, 2007,[6] who married a Chamar) highlighting the horrendous difficulties the pair faced mainly from the Jat family and their kin. Some parents were optimistic about inter-caste marriages and remarked that they want their children to be happy: 'It does not matter who they marry as long they are happy.' Such comments clearly show the high level of acculturation of some Indian parents – which is advocated by many politicians in the UK (Ghuman, 2003).

The young people of Indian origin mixed freely in the schools studied and formed friendships across caste barriers, but when it came to choosing marriage partners their responses were mixed. Some students said they do not want to upset their parents and would marry within their caste and roughly an equal number remarked they would choose their own partners. The sample in our research is small so the findings have to be interpreted with caution, but there is hope that within a generation marriages would be based on individual choice. Some teachers commented that dating is quite common amongst Indian students and most parents know about it but do not want to confront their young people and make an issue of it. I could not, however, establish whether dating was inter-caste or otherwise. My guess is that inter-caste dating is quite common, though few may materialize into marriages, because of the weight of family and kinship traditions against such unions. From the interview data it appears that inter-caste marriages have increased somewhat and continue to do so, as an individualistic mode of seeing the world replaces the collectivist one, in which family and community play a major part (Ghuman, 2003).

Family and Kinship Networking

The chain immigration of Indian people's relatives, friends, and co-villagers has led to the formation of enclaves and networks which are to be found in Coventry (Foleshill), Birmingham (Handsworth and Sparkbrook), and other big cities in the UK (see Chapter 3). The chief purpose of such networks is to stay in touch, weekend visiting, and gathering on family occasions and at religious ceremonies.

---

6   According to her account many marriages in the South Asian community are forced rather than arranged. Honour killing is sometimes concealed as a natural or accidental death. But an in-depth research by Pande (2009) paints a complex picture: ranging from traditionally arranged to semi-arranged and free choice marriages. She emphasizes that arranged should not be understood as forced.

As discussed in Chapter 3, studies by Anwar (1979) and Shaw (2000) describe in a vivid way how the extensive networks of Pakistani Muslims in England are maintained through the organization of religious events such as *vartan bhangi*. Likewise, Dalit communities are close knit and social visiting and meetings at *bhavans* and temples reinforce the bonds of *biraderi* and caste. At engagement and marriage ceremonies invitations are mainly confined to caste *biraderi* (kith and kin). In our child-rearing study (Dosanjh and Ghuman, 1997) we found that children learn their religion and caste both formally and informally from their families in their day-today interaction with relatives and attendance at places of worship. Thus caste divisions are *de facto* nurtured and perpetuated by social networking. The data from family interviews and observations at temples and community centres confirm such a conclusion.

Schooling and Educational Matters

Teachers, parents, and community leaders in the study were almost unanimous in asserting that the school examination performance of Dalit young people is no different from their Indian peers of high castes (Chapter 5). At the same time it was noted from previous research on this topic that Indian young people perform significantly higher than any other ethnic groups, except students of Chinese origin; and that Indian girls show a higher rate of success than boys, just like their girl peers in other ethnic groups (Ghuman, 2003; Gillborn and Mirza, 2000; *Guardian*, 2010; DFES, 2005: 13).

The theories of Ogbu (1995) and Suarez-Orozco and Suarez-Orozco (2001) offer sound explanations for the success of some minority ethnic communities in the US and UK. This vindicates the claims of Dalit activists (CasteWatch, 2010) that if their children and young people are given equal opportunities they are capable of attaining examination success on a par with their counterparts of high castes. This also strengths their view that in India Dalit young people do not perform as well as their high-caste peers because of the poor facilities in public schools (state schools) which their offspring attend (see Chapter 3 for detailed discussion), and due to caste prejudice and discrimination. They go on to defend their right[7] to have 25 per cent (up to 50 per cent now) seats reserved in institutions of higher education, and universities to redress their disadvantaged position. A similar percentage of jobs is available to them in provincial and central government offices and they want this extended to a fast-growing private sector. Some scholars

---

7   Singh writes (2005: 238): 'Those who know social history of this country know it for sure that the socially degraded, odious and economically miserable life of either backwards or the Dalits has no parallel in any society outside India ... Almost all the domestic servants, wage labourers, beggars, rag pickers, rickshaw pullers, slum and pavement dwellers, manual and menial workers, bonded labourers, street vendors and the toiling millions ... are no other than those belonging to lower and intermediary castes.'

(see *Economic Times*, 2006; Shah, 1996) argue that the reservation of jobs would lead to a lowering of standards in professional jobs such as information technology and thereby compromise India's ability to compete in the world market. At a grass roots level this has caused a great deal of tension between Dalits and other caste people (see Chapter 2). It seems to be, then, primarily a debate over the severe competition for scarce resources in the vastly expanded population of India which now exceeds one billion. This controversy is similar to the one which raged in the US until recently on affirmative action for African-Americans and other disadvantaged minorities.

None of the students in the study indicated that their identity is caste based. A number of them chose British-Indian or British-Asian as their identity. Hyphenated identity is a popular choice amongst Indian-origin young people in Canada and the US (Ghuman, 2003) and some other ethnic groups in North America, for example, African-Americans. However, Chamar young people were quite happy with, even proud of, their caste position and argued that their community is as good as any other Indian community in the UK. A few said they have been jokingly called names, but nothing serious has happened in their school. However, we offered an analysis of humour based on Allport's theory of stereotypes and suggested that jokes can be quite potent in perpetuating and reinforcing prejudice and discrimination (see Chapter 5)

All the teachers and head teachers interviewed for the project were of the view that caste has never been a problem in their school (Chapter 5). They have never had a complaint from parents on this matter and students mix well in their multicultural schools, although ethnicity plays a part in it. Both the head teachers in the project argued that they realize it is an issue for the Indian community, because separate places of worship do exist and marriages are organized along caste lines. However, they do not think it could be dealt with in the school by formulating anti-caste policies. All the teachers in the study were of a similar view and felt that casteism cannot be equated with racism as the latter is a broader problem and touches all students and the wider population.[8] However, some teachers were of the opinion, as were some students, that it can be included in the school curricula (religious education, history) to impart to students some understanding of the caste system. Some parents in the interview also suggested this type of approach. One Dalit activist said that caste is a deep psychological problem with many Indians in that both victims and oppressors deny caste divisions as a social reality and even think it is a personal problem. This is a valid point to make since a few students did remark 'No problem, but it is a joke.' From my extensive observation and analysis of empirical data, I conclude that all students will benefit from learning

---

8   Dalit Solidarity (2010) and Castwatch UK (2010) have produced evidence to show that there are cases of caste bullying in schools and that casteism can be equated with racism. Further discussion follows presently. Also see the findings in the NIESR Report (Metcalf, and Rolfe, 2010) which suggests that caste bullying and harassment in schools can be better dealt with by including caste in the Single Equality Act 2010.

the history and the working of caste stratification and divisions. It will especially help students of Indian/South Asian origin to understand objectively an important legacy of their past social history. In my view, caste is an important element in fully understanding Hinduism and its basic principles (see Chapter 1) and can be taught in the school curriculum. It can be discussed when teachers cover the two other important topics of racism and sexism in personal health and social education (PHSE) courses.

Dalit organizations (websites of: ACDA, 2010; CasteWatch, 2010; International Dalit Solidarity, 2010) have mounted a sustained campaign to include caste discrimination in the Single Equality Bill in the British Parliament. Their argument is that caste discrimination is to be found amongst the Indian diaspora and it is likely to get worse as some Indian-based companies start to operate in the UK. It is argued that it is as pernicious as racism[9] and we need a framework of law to address it. However, the evidence presented to the House of Lords Committee to support their case was considered not robust and comprehensive, therefore the outgoing Labour government (see Chapter 3) has commissioned large-scale research to find out the extent and scale of caste discrimination in employment and the delivery of services.[10] However, such a law would acknowledge two important social realities: caste divisions do exist and might lead to discrimination as Indian employers are extending their activities in the UK; and that British society does not tolerate prejudice and discrimination based on race, gender, religion, or caste.[11] The schools then would be obliged to have a policy on casteism on a par with racism and sexism. Although our small sample of educationalists is not in favour of it, they perhaps will not object to it either. The practical problems of policy making on this issue can be considerable, for example, staff training and resources. But the real difficulty lies in the fact that schools may be asked to address too many social issues and thus they might be detracted from pursuing their main objective of preparing students for examinations. Research indicates (Ghuman, 1980; Verma and Ashworth, 1986) that the vast majority of Indian, and indeed other parents, want their children to gain success in school examinations so that they can compete with advantage in the job market. Ethnic minority parents' own personal experiences have taught them that educational qualifications are the key to obtaining well-paid jobs and for social mobility. Many of them are of the view (maybe mistakenly) that they can teach their children social and religious history, and indeed their community languages. However, the important point to consider is that school is the only agency, unlike home and places of worship, which all

9   A teacher interviewed for this project argued that teachers raised similar objections when racism was discussed in the 1970s (also see Gillborn, 1995).

10   The report by NIESR suggests that there is a strong case to include caste discrimination in the Single Equality Act.

11   According to one report (Telegraph.co.uk, 2009) the UN Committee on Human Rights might declare caste discrimination as pernicious as race and thus draw attention of the wider world to the issue. But the Indian government is opposed to it.

children and young people are obliged to attend. Schools, therefore, offer golden opportunities to discuss and debate social and cultural issues with some degree of objectivity. School is an ideal place where students can learn to appreciate cultural and religious differences held by diverse sections of society.

Dalit organizations have also encouraged the development of drama and music to counter the negative effect of caste prejudice. The play *Fifth Cup* brilliantly displays the inhumanity of caste prejudice and has attracted large audiences in UK theatres. Likewise, music by various groups has universal themes of brotherhood and humanity in which all young people join and rejoice. A Chamar boy told me:

> I am a DJ and go to birthday and other special occasions and play all sorts of music. Every one joins in … there are a few who want to listen to Jat bhangra music so I play it. It might upset some people but I think it is a joke, because I also play music where Chamars say they are proud of being what they are.

In Uttar Pradesh, India, the government of Mayawati has set up a special committee to promote Dalit literature and art. She wants her followers to be proud of their Dalit heritage and identity and has commissioned artists to revive myths, folk tales, and legends of the heroic deeds of their ancestors. Narayan (2006) has spent several years studying this social and cultural phenomenon as discussed in Chapter 2 of the book.

Individualism *vis-à-vis* Collectivism

We alluded to the indvidualism vs. collectivism values system in Chapter 4 of the book. It is an important conceptual framework which differentiates traditional societies from those of the West. We did not set out to conduct research on this topic, but from our empirical data it can be inferred that young people of the third-generation are now opting for a style of life which can be described as individualistic. Their conversation and dialogue with the researcher reflects this. They often referred to their own aspirations, struggles, and anxieties without unduly worrying over the concerns of their parents or kinsfolk. They worry about their friendships, leisure time activities, and studies like their white peers. Those young people whose both parents (or one of them) were/was born in this country receive great encouragement to consider their own wishes and aspirations and happiness rather than worry unduly about the family. We also infer from the data that they are pursuing a strategy of integration with British culture rather than assimilation of or separation from the host society. It is important to note that they are not alienated young people and fully appreciate the diversity of British society. The integration mode of acculturation offers the best strategy of accommodating the norms of British society in that it combines the values of family and school and wider society (see Berry and Sabatier, 2010).

Indian Connections

Indian parents and their children frequently visit their extended family and relatives and nurture mixed feelings about their 'old home'/parents' country. Most of the young people in the study enjoyed their stay in India and saw some of the historic and religious buildings and monuments along with impressive modern developments. Dalit young people came face-to-face with the hard realties of caste segregation in their villages (Chapter 5, and Case Study 3). They saw how their kith and kin live in a separate part of their village, and some still live in enclaves on the village boundaries. They felt real pain when their relatives fell ill and could not afford the services of a qualified doctor. Instead, they have to be content with home remedies or go to a village *desi hakim*. They talked to their peers about their experiences of shortages of basic foodstuffs, lack of educational resources, rampant corruption amongst politicians, police and bureaucrats. They were dismayed by all this and relieved to come back and thankful for the opportunities offered in the UK (see Case Study 3). For some, India offered good opportunities to work because of its expanding economy and the progress of their communities at a political level. They felt inspired by the success of Mayawati, the first Dalit woman Chief Minister (Chapter 2) and by Meira Kumar the first Dalit Speaker of the Lok Sabha (Indian parliament). Many young people think that they can empower their community in India with useful new skills and a motivation to succeed. Retired Indian Dalits in the UK have already set up charities and/or are supporting charitable work in hospitals, schools, and *ashrams* for children in India. They also serve as an inspiration to their communities in India when they relate their material success and high achievement in professions such as law, teaching (university professors), and politics (MPs). Some have run very successful businesses and are still active and also doing voluntary work.

Reservation for Dalits and OBCs

The implementation of the Mandal Commission's recommendations in 1990 on the reservation of government posts and jobs and places in educational establishments for the OBCs sparked a bitter debate amongst its advocates and adversaries (R.B.S, Verma, 2005). There were violent protests by high-caste students and even a few cases of self-harm and self-immolation. The report recommended that in addition to reservation (of 22 per cent) for Scheduled Castes and Scheduled Tribes (former Untouchables) the OBCs should be awarded 27 per cent of the places. But the reservation should not exceed 50 per cent of the total places in universities, technical and medical colleges. Likewise the same principle should apply to government posts and subsequent promotion. Successive Indian governments (from 1990 to 1991) issued executive memoranda accepting the main recommendations of the report. But these were challenged in the Supreme Court and the issue became a landmark constitutional legal case: *Indra Sawhney v. Union of India*. The Court delivered its majority verdict in November 1991 upholding the Indian government's right to issue executive directives and thus endorsing the main recommendations of the Mandal Commission, with few exceptions (see N. Verma, 2005).[12] We discussed this issue in Chapter 2 and presented the views of Jats and Dalits which highlight the tension between the two communities in a village. The riots and social protests following the implementation of the report happened 20 years ago but the landmark Supreme Court's judgment continues to cause anger and bitter resentment amongst high-caste people on the one hand and vindication of a just cause by Dalits and OBCs on the other.

Further Research and Projects

There is a paucity of research on the above discussed issues in the UK, though a great deal is being mounted in India by both Indian and Western scholars. Indeed, comprehensive research on all aspects of Dalit diasporas' lives is needed. This can range from topics in education such as achievement, vocational aspirations, friendship patterns, home school links, to in-depth research on caste identities. Perhaps the most rewarding project would be with over-16s who have left school or have entered institutions of higher education. It is clear that caste friendships come under strain at this level when decisions on marriage and social networking loom large. Dhanda's (2008) research is a very good example of ground-breaking study on over-16s and she is now carrying out a large-scale project on various aspects of Dalits' lives in the UK.

Some in-depth research has already been carried out on *bhavans* and Valmiki temples (Kalsi, 1992; Knott 1994; Nesbit, 1990) but more is needed to find out the extent of formal and informal rituals and practices at religious places which tend to encourage caste exclusivity or in some cases caste unity. Dalit networking across country has been forged by electronic media and it would be most interesting to know how this strategy is impacting on the lives of young people in India and abroad. Inter-caste marriages are one of the ways forward for the elimination of caste consciousness (Ambedkar, 1997) and in this field too we need new studies. Follow-up work on inter-caste marriages and offspring of such unions would be most illuminating. Thus, there are great research opportunities open to scholars and students to enrich the existing literature on ethnic minority

---

12 The reader's attention is directed to an excellent discussion on this issue by Keane (2007: 3–158). Keane concludes his discussion: 'Reservations have contributed enormously to the uplift of the Scheduled Castes and Scheduled Tribes and Other Backward Classes … Untouchability is but a symptom of caste; that reservations do not tackle the caste system itself; and that the root cause inequality in India is the caste system, which was not abolished in 1950' (p. 157).

communities by including Dalit people in their samples. To conclude this chapter we present a discussion[13] on the present controversial topic of Dalit assertion in North India.

---

13   During my extended stay in India, I listened to a discussion on a Zee Punjabi TV programme relating to a statement made by Ravidasi in Benares about the inauguration of a new religion. The participants were Dr Ronki Ram, a reader at the Punjab University and Dr Grewal, an Emeritus Professor of history. The latter was defending the Sikh perspective that their religion is all-inclusive. He argued that Jats who now control the SGPC and are the dominant community in the Punjab were once considered Shudra until the 18th century. They have raised their social position and status because they embraced Sikhism and rebuffed the high-caste people by telling them that they are as good, if not better, than they are. The Sikh practice of *langar* and *pangat* were initiated to undermine and eliminate untouchability. Dr Ronki Ram gave an historical account of the Dalit movement starting with Mangoo Ram. He suggested that this is the revival of Ram's pledge to start a new religion of Ad Dharam. The person advocating the Chamar cause argued that we do not want equality once a fortnight in a *gurdwara*, but on day-to day basis. *Langar* and *pangat* are good concepts but they do not affect economic implications. Grewal argued that Sikhism provides the spirit and motivation for equality and economic reforms should flow from there. Cynics suggest that this is a ploy by Mayawati and others to extend their influence from UP to the neighbouring states. The debate ended up inconclusively. (6 February 2009 Zee Punjabi TV, broadcast at 7 o'clock).

Bibliography

Abbas, T. (2004), *The Education of British South Asians: Ethnicity, Capital and Class Structure* (London: Palgrave Macmillan).

Allport, G. (1954), *The Nature of Prejudice* (Cambridge, MA: Addison-Wesley).

Ambedkar, B. (1997), *The Buddha and his Dhama* (Nagpur: Budha Bhoomi Publication).

Ambedkar, B. (N.D), *The Untouchables: Who Were They and Why They Became Untouchables* (Jalandhar: Bheem Patrika Publications).

Anwar, M. (1979), *The Myth of Return: Pakistanis in Britain* (London: Heinemann).

Baker, C. (1995), *Foundations of Bilingualism* (Clevedon: Multilingual Matters).

Ballard, R. (1994), 'Differentiation and Disjunction Among the Sikhs' in *Desh Pardesh: The South Asian Presence in Britain* (London: Hurst & Company).

Barrett, M. (2007), *Children's Knowledge, Beliefs and Feelings about Nations and National Groups* (Hove: Psychology Press).

Bayly, S. (1999), *Caste, Society and Politics in India from the Eighteenth Century to the Modern Age* (Cambridge: Cambridge University Press).

Bellin, W. (1995), 'Psychology and Bilingualism', in B.M. Jones and P.A.S. Ghuman (eds) *Bilingualism and Identity* (Cardiff: University of Wales Press).

Berry, W.J. (1997), 'Immigration, Acculturation, and Adaptation', *Applied Psychology: An International Journal*, 46(1), 5–68.

Berry, W.J. and Sabatier, C. (2010), 'Acculturation, Discrimination, and Adaptation among Second Generation Immigrant Youth in Montreal and Paris', *International Journal of Intercultural Relations*, 34, 191–207.

Beteille, A. (1996), *Caste, Class and Power: Changing Patterns of Stratification in a Tanjore Village* (Delhi: Oxford University Press).

Bhachu, P. (1985), *Twice Migrants: East African Sikh Settlers in Britain* (London: Tavistock).

Bhatia, B. (2006), 'Dalit Rebellion against Untouchability in Chakwada, Rajasthan', *Contribution to Indian Sociology*, 40(1), 29–61.

Bhatti, G. (1999), *Asian Children at Home and at School* (London: Routledge).

Bhatty, Z. (1976), 'Status of Muslim Women and Social Change', in B.R. Nanda (ed.) *Indian Women: From Purdah to Modernity* (New Delhi: Vikas).

Bilton, T., Bonnett, K., Jones, P., Skinner, D., Stanworth, M. and Webster, A. (1997), *Introductory Sociology* (Basingstoke: Palgrave).

Bob, C. (2007), 'Dalit Rights Are Human Rights: Caste Discrimination, International Activism, and the Construction of a New Human Rights Issue', *Human Rights Quarterly*, 29, 167–93.

Brown, K. (1988), *The Essential Teachings of Hinduism* (London: Rider).

Burra, N. (1996), 'Buddhism, Conversion and Identity: A Case Study of Mahar', in N.M. Srinivas (ed.) *Caste: Its Twentieth Century Avatar* (New Delhi: Penguin Books India).

Chakravarti, U. (2003), *Gendering Caste: Through a Feminist Lens* (Kolkata: Stree Dalit Solidarity Network, 2006).

Chirkov, V. (guest editor) (2009), *International Journal of Intercultural Relations*, 33(2), whole issue.

Dalit Solidarity Network (2006), *Caste Discrimination in the UK* (London: Dalit Solidarity Network).

Davey, A. (1983), *Learning to be Prejudiced: Growing up in Multi-ethnic Britain* (London: Edward Arnold).

Deliege, R. (1999), *The Untouchables of India* (Oxford: Berg).

Devine, G.P. (2005), 'Breaking the Prejudice: Allport's Inner Conflict', in F.J Dovidio, P. Glick, and Rudman, L.A. (ed.) *On the Nature of Prejudice: Fifty Years after Allport* (Oxford: Blackwell).

Dhanda, M. (2009), 'Punjabi Dalit Youth: Social dynamics of transitions in Identity', *Contemporary South Asia*, 17(1), 47–64.

Dosanjh, J.S. and Ghuman, P.A.S. (1997), 'Punjabi Childrearing in Britain: Development of Identity, Religion and Bilingualism', *Childhood: A Global Journal of Child Research*, 4(3), 285–304.

Dosanjh, J.S. and Ghuman, P.A.S. (1999), *Child-Rearing Practices of Ethnic Minorities* (Clevedon: Multilingual Matters).

Dovidio, F.J., Glick, P. and Rudman, A.L. (2005), *On the Nature of Prejudice: Fifty Years after Allport* (Oxford: Blackwell).

Duggal, K. (1988), *Philosophy and Faith of Sikhism* (Honesdale: Himalayan International Institute of Yoga Science and Philosophy of the USA).

Dumont, L. (2004), *Homo Hierarchicus: The Caste System and Its Implications* (Oxford: Oxford University Press).

Embree, T.A. (1958 ed.), *Sources of Indian Tradition: Volume One: From the Beginning to 1800* (New York: Columbia University Press).

Encyclopaedia Britannica (2004), Standard Edition 2004 CD-ROM.

Eysenck, H. (1971), *Race, Intelligence and Education* (London: Temple Smith).

Gaag, N. (2005), 'Caste Out', *New International*, 380, 1–7.

Gandhi, M. (1927), *An Autobiography: The Story of My Experiments with Truth* (Ahmedabad: Navajivan).

Gandhi, M. (1954), *The Removal of Untouchability* (Ahmedabad: Navjivan).

Ghuman, P.A.S. (1975), *The Cultural Context of Thinking: A Comparative Study of Punjabi and English Boys* (Slough: National Foundation For Educational Research).

Ghuman, P.A.S. (1980), 'Bhattra Sikhs in Cardiff: Family and Kinship Organization', *New Community*, 8(2), 308–16.

Ghuman, P.A.S. (1994), *Coping with Two Cultures: British Asians and Indo-Canadian Adolescents* (Clevedon: Multilingual Matters).

Ghuman, P.A.S. (1999), *Asian Adolescents in the West* (Leicester: British Psychological Society).

Ghuman, P.A.S. (2000), 'Acculturation of South Asian Adolescents in Australia', *British Journal of Educational Psychology*, 70(3), 305–16.

Ghuman, P.A.S. (2003), *Double Loyalties: South Asian Adolescents in the West* (Cardiff: University of Wales Press).

Gibson, M.A. (1988), *Accommodation without Assimilation* (Ithaca and London: Cornell University Press).

Gillborn, D. and Mirza, S.H. (2000), *Educational Inequality: Mapping Race, Class and Gender* (London: Office for Standards in Education).

Gillborn, D. (1995), *Racism and Antiracism in Real Schools* (Buckingham: Open University Press).

Gombrich, F.R. (1988), *Theravada Buddhism: A Social History from Ancient Benares to Modern Colombo* (London: Routledge).

Gombrich, F.R. (1988), 'Karma' (unpublished paper: Oxford: Oxford University).

Guha (2007), *India After Gandhi: The History of the Largest Democracy* (New York: Harper-Collins).

Hall, D.K. (2002), *Lives in Translation: Sikh Youth as British Citizens* (Philadelphia: University of Pennsylvania Press).

Hardtmann, E. (2003), *Our Fury is Burning: Local Practice and Global Connections in the Dalit Movement* (Stockholm: Stockholm Studies in Social Anthropology).

Hess, L. (1983) *The Bijak of Kabir* (San Francisco: North Point Press).

Jadhav, N. (2002), *Untouchables: My Family's Triumphant Journey out of the Caste System in Modern India* (New York: Scribner).

Jodhka, S. (2004), 'Sikhism and the Caste Question: Dalits and Their Politics in Contemporary Punjab', *Contribution to Indian Sociology*, 38, 165–92.

Joshi, B. (1982), *Democracy in Search of Equality: Untouchable Politics and Indian Social Change* (Delhi: Hindustan Publishing Corporation).

Juergensmeyer, M. (1982), *Religion as Social Vision: The Movement against Untouchability in 20th-Century Punjab* (Berkeley: University of California Press).

Kalsi, S. (1992), *The Evolution of a Sikh Community in Britain* (Leeds: Community Religions Project, University of Leeds).

Keane, D. (2007), *Caste-based Discrimination in International Rights Law* (Aldershot: Ashgate).

Keer, D. (2005), *Dr. Ambedkar: Life and Mission* (Mumbai: Popular Parkashan).

Klostermaier, K. (1999), *Buddhism: A Short Introduction* (Oxford: One Word).

Knott, K. (1986), *Hinduism in Leeds: A Study of Religious Practice in the Indian Hindu Community and in Hindu-Related Groups* (Leeds: Community Religions Project, University of Leeds).

Knott, K. (1994), 'The Gujarati Mochi in Leeds: From Leather Stockings to Surgical Boots and Beyond', in R. Ballad. (ed.), *Desh Pardesh* (London: Hurst and Company).

Leslie, J. (2003), *Authority and Meaning in Indian Religions: Hinduism and the Case Of Valmikis* (Aldershot: Ashgate).

Leyens, J., Yzerbyt, V. and Schadron, G. (1994), *Stereotype and Social Cognition* (London: Sage).

Mahar, M.J. (1972 ed.), *The Untouchables in Contemporary India* (Tucson: University of Arizona Press).

Mendelsohn, O. and Vicziany, M. (1998), *The Untouchables* (Cambridge: Cambridge University Press).

Metcalf, H. and Rolfe, M. (NIESR Report, 2010), *Caste Discrimination and Harassment in Great Britain* (London: National Institute of Economic and Social Research).

Michael, M. (1999), *Dalits in Modern India* (New Delhi: Vistaar Publications).

Misra, M. (2003), *Vishnu's Crowded Temple: India since Great Rebellion* (London: Allen Lane).

Mukerji, S. (2005), *Our World: Then and Now* (New Delhi: Bharti Bhawan).

Narayan, B. (2006), *Women Heroes and Dalit Assertion in North India* (New Delhi: Sage).

Nesbit, E. (1990), 'Religion and Identity: The Valmiki Community in Coventry', *New Community,* 16(2), 261–74.

Nesbitt, E. (2000), *The Religious Lives of Sikh Children: A Coventry Based Study* (Leeds: Community Religious Project, University of Leeds).

Ogbu, J.U. (1995), 'Cultural Problems in Minority Education: Their Interpretation and Consequences, Part One: The Theoretical Background', *The Urban Review*, 27(3), 190–205.

Olivelle, P. (2004), *The Law Code of Manu* (Oxford: Oxford University Press).

Omvedt, G. (2003), *Buddhism in India* (New Delhi: Sage Publications India Ltd).

Padmasuri (1997), *But Little Dust: Life amongst the 'Ex-untouchables' Buddhists of India* (Birmingham: Windhorse Publications).

Pande, R. (2009), 'Arranged Marriage and British Asians', *Conference Abstracts* 11 June (Guildford: University of Surrey).

Pandharinth, H.B. (1993), *Hindu Social Organization: A Study in Socio-Psychological and Ideological Foundations* (Mumbai: Popular Prakashan).

Parekh, B. (1986), 'The Structure of Authority within the Indian Family', in K.A. Brah (ed.) *Working with Asian Young People* (London: National Association for Asian Youth).

Pawde, K. (1995), 'The Position of Dalit Women in Indian Society', in D. Bhagwan and M. James (eds) *Dalit Solidarity* (Delhi: ISPCK).

Ports, A. and Rumbaut, G.R. (2001), *Legacies: The Story of the Immigrant Second Generation* (Berkeley: Russell Sage Foundation and University of California Press).

Puri, H.K. (2003), 'Scheduled Castes in Sikh Community: A Historical Perspective', *Economic and Political Weekly*, 38(26), 2693–713.

Quigley, D. (1993), *The Interpretation of Caste* (Oxford: Oxford University Press).

Quigley, D. (1994), 'Is a Theory of Caste Still Possible?', in M. Searle-Chaterjee and U. Sharma (eds) *Contextualising Caste* (Oxford: Blackwell).

Rudimen, F.W. (2003), 'Critical History of the Acculturation Psychology of Assimilation, Separation, Integration, and Marginalization', *Review of General Psychology*, 7, 3–37.

Said, E.W. (1995), *Orentialism: Western Conceptions of the Orient* (London: Penguin Books).

Sanghera, J. (2007), *Shame* (London: Hodder and Stoughton).

Selvam, S. (2000), *Caste and Class in India in the Late Twentieth Century* (Lampeter: Edwin Mellen).

Sen, A. (2005), *The Argumentative Indian* (London: Allen Lane).

Ram, R. (2004), 'Untouchability, Dalit Consciousness, and the Ad Dharm Movement in Punjab', *Contribution to Indian Sociology*, 38, 323–48.

Ram, R. (2004), 'Untouchability in India with a Difference: Ad Dharm, Dalit Assertion and Caste Conflict in Punjab', *Asian Survey*, 44(4), 895–912.

Seymour-Smith, C. (1986), *Macmillan Dictionary of Anthropology* (London: Macmillan Press).

Shah, M.A. (1996), 'Job Reservation and Efficiency', in M.N. Srinivas (ed.) *Caste: Its Twentieth Century Avatar* (New Delhi: Penguin Books).

Sharma, A. (2005), 'Dr. B.R. Ambedkar on the Aryan Invasion and the Emergence of the Caste System in India', *Journal of the American Academy of Religion*, 73(3), 843–70.

Shaw, A. (2000), *Kinship and Continuity: Pakistani Families in Britain* (Amsteldijk: Harwood Academic Publishers).

Singh, G. and Tatla, D. (2006), *Sikhs in Britain: The Making of a Community* (London: Zed Books).

Singh, K. (1999), *A History of the Sikhs: Volume 2: 1839–1988* (New Delhi: Oxford University Press).

Singh, J.P. (2005), 'Caste System: A Cultural Mechanism for Social and Economic Deprivation', in H.S. Verma, *The OBCs and the Ruling Classes in India* (New Delhi: Rawat Publications).

Smith, D. and Tomlinson, S. (1989), T*he School Effect: A Study of Multi-racial Comprehensives* (London: Policy Studies Institute).

Srinivas, M. (1996 ed.), *Caste: Its Twentieth Century Avatar* (New Delhi: Penguin Books).

Srinivas, M. (2002), *Collected Essays* (New Delhi: Oxford University Press).

Sharma, R. (2008), *The Caste System: A Report* (London: Hindu Council UK).

Suarez-Orozco, C. and Suarez-Orozco, M.M. (2001), *Children of Immigrants* (Cambridge: Harvard University Press).

Stopes-Roe, M. and Cochrane, R. (1990), *Citizens of this Country: The Asian British* (Clevedon: Multilingual Matters).

Tajfel, H. (1982 ed.), *Social Identity and Intergroup Relations* (Cambridge: Cambridge University Press).

Tharamangalam, J. (1996), 'Caste among Christians in India', in M.N. Srinivas (ed.) *Caste: Its Twentieth Century Avatar* (New Delhi: Penguin Books).

Tomlinson, S. (1998), 'New Inequalities? Educational Markets and Ethnic Minorities', *Race, Ethnicity and Education*, 1(2), 207–23.

Triandis, C.H. (1991), 'Individualism and Collectivism', Invited Address to the International Association for Cross-Cultural Society (IACCP) Conference, Debrecen, Hungary, 4–7 July, 1991.

Verma, G.K. and Ashworth, B. (1986), *Ethnicity and Educational Achievement in British Schools* (London: Macmillan).

Verma, H.S. (2005 ed.), *The OBCs and the Ruling Classes in India* (Jaipur and New Delhi: Rawat Publications).

Verma, N. (2005), 'Indra Sawhney, Before and After: The Historic Journey of a Milestone Case on Compensatory Discrimination in India', in Verma, H.S., *The OBCs and the Ruling Classes in India* (New Delhi: Rawat Publications).

Verma, R.B.S. (2005), 'Creamy Layer among the OBCs, Operationalization and Current Status', in Verma, H.S., *The OBCs and the Ruling Classes in India* (New Delhi: Rawat Publications).

Vernon, P.E. (1969), *Intelligence and Cultural Environment* (London: Methuen).

Vernon, P.E. (1982), *The Abilities and Achievement of Orientals in North America* (New York: Academic Press).

Weber, M. (1958), Religion of India: The Sociology of Hinduism and Buddhism (New Delhi: Munshiram Manoharlal).

Weinreich, P. (2009), '"Enculturation" not "acculturation": Conceptualising and assessing identity processes in migrant communities'. *International Journal of Intercultural Relations*, 33(2), 124–39.

Zelliot, E. (1972), 'Gandhi and Ambedkar: A Study in Leadership', in M.J. Mahar, (ed.) *The Untouchables in Contemporary India* (Tucson: University of Arizona Press).

Zhang. Z. (2009), Education, Migration, and Cultural Capital in the Chinese Diaspora: Transnational Students between Hong Kong and Canada, *International Education*, 38(2), 104–9.

Websites

ACDA (2009): http://www.acdauk.org.uk (accessed 2 March, 2010).

Castewatch UK: http://www.castewatchUK org (accessed 10 October, 2010).

Census of India: http://:www.census of India (accessed 10 July, 2010).

Dalit Solidarity Network (2006): *No Escape: Caste Discrimination in the UK.* http://dsnuk.org/ (accessed 8 October, 2008).

Dalit Solidarity (2010): http:///dsnuk.org/

DFES (2005): *Ethnicity and Education: The Evidence on Minority Ethnic Pupils.* http//www.standards.dfes.gov.uk/ethnic minorities (accessed 2 April, 2010).

Hobson, K: http://www.britishempire.co.uk/ article/castesystem.htm (accessed 4 April, 2010).

Human Rights Watch: http//:www.org/reports/1999/India (accessed 10 May, 2009).

International Conference on Dalit Solidarity (2000): http://www. voiceofdalitinternational.org/wwd.html#ddc (accessed 10 October, 2008).

International Dalit Solidarity Network (2005): *Annual Report* (website: International Dalit Solidarity Network), http://isdn.org/fileadmin/user_ folder/2005ANREPORT.pdf (accessed 10 May, 2010).

International Dalit Solidarity Network: *I'm Dalit, How Are You?* (film) http:www. idsn.org/movie/dalit.htm (accessed 23 August, 2007).

Telegraph.co.uk (2009): http//:www.telegraph.co.uk/world news (accessed 10 July, 2010).

Yahoo News India (2010): Ravidassia Community Part of Sikh faith: SGPC. http//: www.in.news.yahoo.com. (accessed 13 February, 2010).

Newspaper articles

Economic Times (2006), 'Debate: Is Affirmative Action Limited to Quotas?' (2 May, 2002).

Economic Times (2009), 'Indian-born MP Wants Caste Bias Banned in Britain' (12 May, 2006).

Guardian (2006), 'Violence Feared in Indian Caste Row' (17 May, 2006): 23.

Guardian (2006), 'Indian Leader Likens Caste System to Apartheid Regime' (28 December, 2006).

Guardian (2010), 'Race, Class and a Society Divided' (11 October, 2010).

Hindu (2010), 'Untouchability Still Prevalent in Rural Gujarat' (29 January, 2010).

Jag Bani (2006), 'Absent Teachers' (28 November, 2006).

Sunday Times India (2010), 'Real Caste India Still Long Way Off' (31 January, 2010).

The Times (2008), 'Queen of the Untouchables' Defies Bribery Charges to Aim for Top Job (16 January, 2008).

The Times (2009), 'How Queen of the Untouchables May Become the New Kingmaker' (11 April, 2009).

The Times (2010), 'Young Generation Keeps Old Identities Alive with Bhangra Music Tradition', and 'Forbidden Love: No Redress for Couples Divided by Caste' (5 July, 2010).

The Tribune (2007), 'She champions the cause of Dalit women' (3–5, 28 February, 2007).

Appendix A
Six Case Studies

Case Study 1: Retired Captain

This case study is of a successful retired army officer whose family I have known for the last 50 years. He belongs to a Chamar caste but is a *pucka* Sikh who sports a 'full beard and turban.' This is a heart warming story of a man who has attained high status through his own efforts. His father was a farm worker and mother was a housewife but worked as a general helper in farmers' houses. She did a variety of jobs for farmers which included: winnowing, fetching vegetables from farms, helping with washing, and baby sitting. In addition, she raised her own five children, kept two cows and several hens. Though she helped farmers' households generously, she was not allowed to enter their kitchens. Farmers gave her food but it was usually leftovers and she ate it in her own utensils or took it home to share with her family. Although she brought raw vegetables from farms she was not allowed to cook as she was deemed to be polluted, but it was never openly acknowledged. Despite all these insults and slights she was cheerful and held her head high.

The family lived in a mud house consisting of two rooms and an open courtyard with a couple of neem trees. The house was in a separate location called 'Chamarli', where Chamars live separate from the farmers. During the rainy season their house leaked all the time and the family often lived in a damp environment for several days. This caused many illnesses in the family for which they could ill afford to see a doctor or buy medicine. The family relied on traditional remedies to alleviate their ailments. Water for drinking was to be fetched from a well meant for Chamar families only. All the farmers in the village had water pumps in their houses. For calls of nature nearby fields were used. Mustard oil lamps provided poor light in the evening so the family tried to finish their cooking and domestic chores during the day light. The family mixed with their own caste people and marriages were arranged within their own community. Wedding customs required large sums of money which they would have to borrow from their employing farmer and thus the family was in unending debt and had to work for the same farmer: the father and mother worked for the same family for 22 years.

The father worked at least 12 hours a day and there was no such thing as a weekend or annual holidays. He could have days off on religious festivals or when he was not well. His employing farmer provided him with cooked meals three times a day and this was considered to be a perk of the job. Farmers' households, of course, ate better quality food and this was shared with their farm workers. It was a precarious existence as there was no provision for education or medical treatment. The family could not afford to buy new clothes and relied on farmers' old discarded ones.

Thus his parents struggled and saved to send their youngest son (a captain now) to high school. He was a bright, hard-working student and passed his matriculation examination with flying colours. His parents were delighted and thought of sending him to a college. But he preferred to join the Indian Army. There were very few *jawans* (recruits) who had matriculation qualifications, therefore his progress was rapid. He helped his fellow soldiers in a variety of ways such as writing letters home, speaking on their behalf to officers, and so on. He gained rapid promotion and became a junior commissioned officer on his own merits. He loved the army life as it was free of caste discrimination and *jawans* were treated fairly on their merit. He never met any prejudice in the army and people did not bother to ask his caste or religion. He shared all the facilities with his fellow officers and 'there was never any question of eating separately because I belonged to a Chamar caste'. He retired as an honorary captain – a rank awarded to non-commissioned officers to enhance their pay and status.

During our interview he did discuss the situation of his parents who were treated in a demeaning manner by the village farmers. He narrated:

> My father had to have his own eating utensils and drinking glasses and normally sat on the ground/floor when eating or talking to his employer. If he forgot his drinking glasses he has to 'cup' has hand to drink water and ate chappatis with vegetables which he held in his hands. He was at the beck and call of his employer round the clock without any holidays or breaks. My mother was doing all sort of chores for the farmers and was not paid but was given fodder or vegetables for her services ... There was no cash payment for all the work she did. When I think of their lives, it does hurt me but I do not dwell on it. It was accepted at that time (1960s). Thank God those days are over and we can enjoy our freedom from the farmers as there are other openings for our community.[1]

He continued:

> I retired a few years back and my pension is very good and I am better off than many farmers. I am also *Sarpanch* (Headman) of the village Panchayat and receive due respect form all communities. I am invited to farmers' weddings and religious (*bhog*) ceremonies and there is no caste prejudice. It does not mean all is well but there has been a sea change since my childhood in the right direction ... It is more to do with your financial circumstances – your *pucka* house, kids'

---

1   I did not ask any questions on the sexual exploitation of Dalit/Chamar women and he did not raise it either in his conversation with me. But there is plenty of evidence that this was a common practice in the 1950s (see Chapter 3), but it has ceased completely since then.

private education, and access to local executive officers. I have built a *pucka* new house, run a small business where I employ my nephews and nieces, and all my kids have attended private schools and managed to secure well-paid jobs.

On affirmative action for Dalits, his views were somewhat different from the current policy of reservation. He argued:

Now many farmers are poorer than I am but my kids had an advantage over them because of the 'reserved quotas'. This is unfair. I think affirmative policy should be based on income rather than caste ... Otherwise it causes a great deal of tension in the village community. Also, the 'creamy layer' (the top class Dalits) take advantage of this situation whereas poor Dalits and others are more deserving. Dalits who become successful move to cities and forget about the vast majority of people who live in villages and need their leadership.

On Sikh *gurdwaras* he had a great deal to say:

I am a Sikh and proud of it. Now we have three *gurdwaras* in the village and they are along the caste lines. This is wrong in my view. Our gurus preached equality and brotherhood/sisterhood (community of *Khalsas*) irrespective of caste or gender and we are backsliding on that. Likewise we have two cemeteries: one for farmers and the other one for lower castes. Now this is terrible ... Even after death people are to be kept separate. I say this is the twenty-first century and we are living in the middle-ages. As a *Sarpanch* [headman] I have to take action on this grave matter. Young people of the Chamar community are very radical and want complete disengagement from the farmers, but that is wrong. We have to learn to live together ... The big issue is employment. There are not many government jobs and factory work is also limited. [*What about farm work?*] No, they would not do it. Some want to work in the Gulf countries and so on ... Another problem which we have to tackle is widespread use of drugs and alcohol.

I was told by many villagers that this is a real problem and raises a question of law and order in the village. There have been several break-ins in the village and young unemployed people are the suspects.

His views on girls' education are equally enlightening. He gave an answer which has become a common currency in India now: 'You educate a son and this is good for him but if you educate a daughter she would educate the whole family and she will take care of the family.'

I asked him how many marriages in the village have been inter-caste. His reply:

None. There was one inter-caste liaison and that was shunned by parents of both castes. This is not going to happen for a long time despite generous government grants to mixed caste couples. Caste is so much part of our psyche especially in the villages and I do not see the end to this for many generations ... In cities it is less marked and in our Armed forces it is good.

He fondly remembered his service in the Army and in a way regretted having to retire in the village wishing to help his kith and kin. He encountered too many problems and was often frustrated by the lack of co-operation from the caste-ridden village society. He gave an example of installing a basic drainage system in the village for which the village has received a grant from the government. There were quarrels and in-fighting for example about which area should be given priority as it was perceived that funds will dry up after the election of 2009. He is a man of integrity who wants to help all the villagers and be fair to all communities but it is an uphill task. His extended family is very large and his resources do not go far to help with education, marriages, and providing houses.

Case Study 2: G ... Domestic Helper[2]

Most middle-class homes in north Indian cities employ domestic servants/helpers and gardeners from Bihar and Uttar Pradesh (UP). Agricultural labourers (mostly men) also hail from the same regions and have found their way into the Punjab and Haryana. Their women folk often work as domestic servants in farmers' households. Most of them belong to Scheduled Castes (Dalits) and are the poorest section of Indian society. They often work long hours without any formal contracts and are poorly paid. Some writers say that they are exploited both by middlemen and employers. I observed the working-life of a 14-year-old girl who was employed as a domestic servant in a Punjabi household. My notes:

> I have been here for a couple of days and enjoyed Z's hospitality. His house is modern, spacious and the interior design is superb. There are three bedrooms, a lobby, a lounge, and a terrace to sit out. They prefer to keep the house in a sort of semi-darkness. I suppose that is because of the hot sun, although they have air conditioning in the bedrooms. The house is full of beautiful artefacts such as ornaments, carving, and statues. I would say altogether it is a comfortable house with all the modern amenities.
>
> The girl who works in the kitchen is called G ... . She tells me she is from a village in Uttar Pradesh where her parents have a few *kanals* (less than an acre) of land. She has three other sisters and they are also working in middle-class Punjabis' households. Although she has a separate room upstairs, she sleeps in the lobby and is at their beck and call 24 hours. They pay her 1000 Rupees (15 pounds) a month and treat her well. She says she is a Hindu and worships the goddess Laxmi and other Hindu Gods (but I was told she belongs to the Chamar caste). She is provided food but eats separately on her own. She is studying

---

2   My reflective comments and observations appear in italics.

for an examination in her spare time, after 10 p.m. The family thinks they are generous towards her and treat her as a family member. She gets up at 6 o'clock in the morning and usually works without break until the family goes to bed. Her duties are manifold, although the main one is in the kitchen. She has been taught to prepare and cook food for the family and guests. She does the washing up, though general cleaning is carried out by another Dalit woman. Her other duties include: running to the nearby shops, child minding, washing, cleaning shoes, and generally to 'fetch and carry'. The family says that they treat her extremely well and are teaching her to do housework such as cooking, shopping and taking care of people. (*Without domestic help the city would come to a halt, literally. Where do they live? Who takes care of their health and education? Perhaps I should find out.*) I was informed that there is a separate colony outside the city where most of them live and commute to work in the city. By European standards it would appear to be gross exploitation but the family thinks they pay her a decent wage and she is almost part of the family. (*Construction work e.g. road works, gardening, house building are mainly the preserve of 'immigrant' labour from Bihar and UP. This reminded me of Mexican domestics, gardeners, and building workers employed in California.*)

I talked to G … on many occasions. Most of her extended family members (includes, aunties and uncles) live in this city or in Chandigarh. She goes home once a week for a few hours to see her mother and three sisters. Her mother is also doing domestic work and the father is in the construction business. She has learnt household skills from her mother. Her room is upstairs and is stuffed with rejected household things and she hardly has time to tidy it up. She has a separate bathroom.

She will sit her 8th class exams (15+) in mathematics and English in a few months. (*When does she have time to study?*) She does not get tired, the man of the house says, so she can study after 10 p.m. in the evening. She is on her feet all day and does things willingly. The family's youngest is a willful boy who is very demanding and wants G to be his playmate and a servant (*Many Indian families spoil their boys, see,* Dosanjh and Ghuman, 1997). The lady of the house treats her kindly but as her personal servant/assistant. Most of her time is spent in catering to the needs of four people. According to the family, she would like – and in many respects is given – the same privileges as they accord to own daughter. (*Both husband and wife think that NRIs – Non resident Indians – are Euro-centered and have forgotten the real Indian way of thinking in these matters.*)

Their daughter attends a private school and she showed me her text books. Her history book describes the caste system and explains the hierarchy within it. I quote: 'The Dasas were the original inhabitant of India … The highest caste comprised of Brahmins and the Kashatriyas or the king … .The Shudras, comprising the Dasas and those Aryans who disobeyed rules formed the lowest caste' (Mukerji, 2005: 27). No explanation is offered of the caste system and the Untouchables are not even mentioned as outcastes. Such omissions from history books make the Untouchables 'invisible' and they strongly resent this and want to introduce a balanced approach to history teaching.

The man of the house tells me that G is really spoilt. She will not obey his daughter and is jealous of her. 'She does not appreciate what we do for her!' We are paying for her medical treatment (ear infection) and her tuition fee at the *gurdwara* where she is learning new 'skills'. Then he adds: 'I am fed up with these people. My promotion is blocked because of "reservation quota" and then I am not paid too well compared to Dalit officers. In the village the young boys are very radical and they want two "*marlas*" (a plot) of land for their house building and it can start any time. They are jealous of our land.' (*Obviously his outburst shows his frustrations and he finds Dalits a convenient scapegoat. So there is a problem?*) His friend, who belongs to a dominant caste of Jats, wholeheartedly supports this point of view. Of course, the main problem is scarcity of resources at all levels and there is strong competition for employment, promotion and land to build houses. Affirmative action (reservation) to improve the dire poor condition of Dalits has soured the relationship between high and low castes. There have been many 'ugly' incidents where high-caste Hindus and Sikhs have demonstrated against reservation and demanded treatment by ability and objective school grades (*Guardian*, 2006).

Case Study 3: – Pinky³

Pinky is a 21-year-old woman whom I interviewed on three occasions during the last three years. My first interview was when she was in the sixth form three years ago (July, 2007). She was born in England, had her full schooling and university education in the UK and is a very confident and articulate person. In the first interview she insisted many times that she has not encountered any caste problems, but later on told me that there were one or two incidents, not serious though, which reflected the ignorance of some Jat families and other Indians. She lives with her parents and has one brother who attended a very well established grammar school. Her parents live in a semi-detached house in a suburb of a large city. Her mother is a good cook and does not work outside the house. But in India she was very active and ploughed her father's farm with a tractor. Her father is very confident and has well formed opinions on social and political matters pertaining to Indian communities. He is very proud of being a Chamar and says it 'loudly' and in public. He attended a secondary school in England and left at 16 to work in a factory. He says: 'Taxi driving is not very lucrative but it pays the bills. Due to the recession, business is going down and there are too many taxis and people have to eat before taxi rides.' He talked about Mayawati. 'She could be the next prime minister of India', and continued: 'Chamar families have divided loyalties, some are for Smajwadi (Party of Mayawati) some are comrades [*meaning they*

---

3 My thoughts and observations appear in italics.

support communist party of India]. There was a fight between two brothers over who supports which party in my village back in the Punjab'

The interview was not recorded but details were taken down immediately after the meeting.

Pinky insisted that but for a single incident she has not met any caste discrimination. However, she knows it is there: in the *gurdwara*, in marriages and social interaction. According to her this is due to ignorance, and very traditional misguided thinking and attitudes. She argued:

> Guru Gobind Singh [the tenth and the last Sikh Guru] was a great equalizer. He baptized his disciples first and then asked them to baptize him. His disciples came from all castes. Now this is a fact but many Jats do not know this. I had a bad encounter with a Jat girl. She goes: 'Your family belongs to the shoe maker class which is lower than us.' But I said what did your people do? Farmers grow wheat, sugar and the like. So I said you needed shoes and we needed wheat so that is fine. But she says my parents say we are superior to you. I said 'no' to that as our gurus say we are all equal. Recently arrived girls from India are very clued up on the caste system. My parents have not told us a great deal about it. They think they do not want to burden us with this negative aspect of Indian life. But they are very proud of belonging to Chamar caste and have never hidden this from any one. My Dad goes back to India and helps his co-villagers irrespective of their caste or religion. [*She asked me whether I was a Jat and then says my best friends are Jats. I do not know what to make of it*].

She continued:

> In the university most of the students are Asians so we do not face any discrimination from our white peers. There is nothing else to say ... in the university we attend our lectures, do our work, and that is it. Ah, yes … My brother had a nasty experience which upset us a lot for a long time. He is a very good cricket player and used to play with another Indian boy. They were great mates. But then suddenly his friend became 'cold' towards him. The reason is that his parents told him that my brother belongs to an 'unclean' Chamar caste. Then my father had a talk with him and said we are as good as any Jats in all aspects: education, financial security, our house, and land in the Punjab. He has got over it now but he was very upset.

Then she described her encounter with an arranged marriage party who came to meet her and her family:

> I questioned the boy about his degree and experience. Boy's father is in business but computer illiterate? How come I ask? So the whole thing was false. The boy was lying and I was not going to accept that his father is superior to my father [*her father is a taxi driver*]. Boy's father never came to meet us. It was this

boy, his Mum and two sisters. [*Now, she has accepted a boy from the Chamar community who is working in a professional job after graduation*].

She continued:

> I told my parents I will accept their plans for marriage but not a boy from India. I went to India when I was four and then four years ago. I would like to visit again but would not like to live there. I like India but I cannot live there because of corruption and disorder. My Dad's village is good but Mum's village is very poor. There are no facilities. Our people are still working on leather *kunus* [processing raw hides with water and chemicals] and it smells terribly. My Mum's brother says he cannot smell anything because he has lost his sense of smell and his nails are dyed permanently. In my Mum's village people do not have access to a doctor and they rely on folk remedies which do not help them with their ailments. It is all very sad. My father says that all communities in his village work together, and they are generally well off. Many of them are in the Indian army and some have emigrated to the UK and Canada. We mainly socialize within our own community but I do go to my friends' houses. *Goras* [white people] treat all us Asians the same [meaning in a discriminatory way] but we can cope.

My Notes after the Interview

Pinky was frank and talked about social and religious matters facing Indian communities. I did not perceive any difference between her style, her manner and many other Indian girls and women I have interviewed in my research projects (Ghuman, 2003, 1994). She is facing similar problems as her high-caste peers are encountering and dealing with them successfully. The house is moderately furnished but has all the facilities. How would I compare this with say a Jat house? It is vey much like a typical working-class Punjabi house. The wife speaks Punjabi fluently and her style is very similar to her husband's.

(*Mother's education?*) She probably attended a middle school. Last time I visited she was too ill and this time she has hurt her knee and is now comforting her son who is to have an operation on his ear. She talks a great deal about her families in the UK and in the Punjab. I would have liked to interview her but she declined courteously.

Case Study 4: Professional Family[4]

I interviewed Minderjit (not his real name) along with his family in their own home. He has one son and four daughters, though only two were present during

---

4   My observations and comments appear in italics.

the interview. His wife works in local school kitchens. He obtained a degree in chemistry and later became a social service worker. He is proud to be a Valmiki and is active in the CasteWatch movement.

He accompanied his father to Britain in 1961 and had a full education in this country. He studied at two universities and mixed easily with other Indian/Asians and native British. He can be described as comfortably middle-class and follows the life style which goes with it. His house is semi-detached with a very pleasant garden at the back and a small one in the front. He has books on Indian music, art, and literature and on many topics of general interest. He seems to be easy with his caste and Indian identity. He is very articulate and can engage in discussion on a variety of topics and subjects.

His two bright and cheerful daughters attend both attend university. One of them knows about Hinduism and her own caste position but she has never met any form of abuse or rudeness from other Indian students or teachers. The second daughter denies any such knowledge or experience of caste but her father reminds her of difficult times she had with other Asian girls in school. She said it was due to other factors such as she had too many white friends and not because of her caste. Subsequently, discussion drifted to other matters. The father did most of the talking and clearly wanted the best education for his daughters. His only son is not religious and rarely goes to the Valmiki temple. His daughters visit temple more frequently but they do not appear to be too keen. The youngest daughter, who is still at school, is very bright too. She is in the top set for mathematics, science, and games. She also aspires to go to university. Father jokes about their marriages – they can make their own choices and that would save him a lot of expense and effort. [*I am not sure how far he is serious*]

The son is not too bothered about India. He loves it here. He says: 'My friends drink but I do not.' In a way he feels the odd man out in the presence of his three sisters who are encouraged to excel by their father.

The son has just achieved eight GSCE passes and is going for AS level apprenticeship for two years. Then he hopes to study for a degree in 'car engineering'. He was open about his school and seems to be happy about it. He has many Asian and white friends. He has never come across any caste prejudice either from Asian peers or Asian teachers – who are five in number. [*Is there any racism in school?*] 'All Asians get this abuse of being called a Paki.' This abuse is common in his view. He is learning to box and would like to engage in other martial arts to protect himself, but he does not yet know which one. He is allowed out and goes to parties but does not drink or smoke. He surfs the internet and watches bare-knuckle fights. He listens to rap music but does not like bhangra music. He has his own room whereas the girls share. [*My observations: A typically growing teenager, but a pleasant lad, nevertheless. He does not seem to bother about caste matters.*]

Father's Awakening

Minderjit relates his personal experience of caste discrimination:

> I was very friendly with a Brahmin boy at school who is of the same age. We
> were great buddies but the awakening came at K's wedding. I was serving
> samosas when K's mother interrupted me and said would you go to a shop to
> buy some more samosas? I did not know at that time why she asked me to do
> that. But now I realize the reason. I think it was due to my caste affiliation. My
> friend's mother thought that guests might find out that I belong to the Chura/
> Valmiki caste and object to my presence and she wanted me out of the way.
> She was thinking that I might be considered 'polluted' by her guests. In 'old'
> times (meaning the 1960s) people spent time with Asian families and visited
> one another's houses. Now most of my kids' friends are white and do not bother
> about caste. But they should know about it. They are old enough to face it. It did
> not bother them when they were young.

He continued:

> My father valued education but was rather strict, so I rebelled and turned against
> him. My father called me Kumar – a typical Kshatriya name so that I would be
> thought of as belonging to high caste [*his daughters names end with Kaur –
> indicating a Sikh name*]. This has worked well for me and I play along with it
> until I become confident to assert my own identity. Then I say I am a Valmiki
> and my wife is a Mazhabi Sikh.
>
> There was a case in our city where a high-caste Hindu gave his traditional
> interpretation and explanation of the caste system. That caused a furore and we
> mobilized our community and other Dalits were very upset and angry. He had
> to apologize publically for his outburst. This was widely reported in the Press.

My Comments after the Interview:

The family treated me to a meal and talked openly about caste and other matters
I cared to raise. My conclusion is that Minderjit's girls and son do not think caste
is important in their lives and do not expect it to have any adverse effect on their
lives. Their father does not agree, but at the same time he said during the course
of the interview that kids are not bothered! The wife did not say anything, though
she was present during the interview. I did want to ask her a few questions on her
family religion, that is, Sikhism but she appeared to be too submissive and shy to
respond. Therefore I thought it would be inappropriate to embarrass her. He did
most of the talking and his girls chipped in when I asked questions for clarification.

He told me Dalit CasteWatch is an umbrella organization which includes
Ravidasis, Valmikis and others who wish to support it. Its aim is to get rid of caste
divisions and discrimination amongst the Indian diaspora. There are many eminent

people in the Dalit communities including a JP, a recipient of the highest Indian civic award of '*Bharat Ratan*', a prison governor, and so on. He says: 'Given equal opportunities our people are as good as any other Indian community. In India we need reservation in jobs and the promotional ladder because there is still a great deal of prejudice and discrimination against our people.'

Case Study 5: Dalit Woman Living with High-Caste Partner[5]

Parkhas is a 55-year-old divorced woman who has lived with a Jat man for several years, but now they have split up. She is on her own as her children (three boys and two girls) are grown up adults and married. This is an interesting study because of inter-caste relationship.

P was reticent in answering questions about her background. She said: 'Why are people so interested in other people's personal background? After all we are born the same way.' It sounds cruder when you say it in Punjabi. This is Deliege's view (1999: 14): 'Untouchables are ashamed of their social background and try to conceal it whenever possible. To be forced publicly to acknowledge one's caste is humiliating and insulting.'

After assuring her of the completely confidential nature of the exercise she did open up and talked several times about caste and other issues facing Indian communities.

> I was born in a north Indian village to a Chamar family who were small land owners and reasonably well-off by Indian standards. I was a bit of a tomboy as I was strong and played *kabaddi* with boys. My parents did not like this sort of behaviour and married me off to an older man when I was only 16. He had settled in England so I emigrated with him.
>
> I worked in a factory for several years and had my children at the same time. My husband was very possessive and a control freak. He would collect my wages directly from the factory foreman, and also became abusive. He would beat me regularly and made me do all the shopping and housework after my shift in the factory. I became very depressed and for several years I saw a snake sitting by me and that would accompany me everywhere. It was not a maligned creature but good company. I had a guru in India who also counselled and guided me during this crisis.
>
> My parents came to visit me in England and were shocked to see me. I was a mental and physical wreck. They were appalled at the cruel behaviour of my husband. In the past, they dissuaded me from seeking divorce but now they were fully behind me. So we were divorced and I had the custody of my children.

---

5   Text in italics shows my prompts and questioning. All names the narrative have been changed.

Regrettably, my girls were grown up at that time and sought their own future but I am close to my boys.

I moved away from my parents (who had settled in England) to take a lodging in a house nearby and fell in love with a very nice man of Jat caste. Caste has nothing do with our relationship (see the section titled 'P's Partner's Views') as we were both indifferent to such matters. Due to many ailments I had to give up work and I am now on welfare benefits. I am very grateful to this country for the support it has given me and my parents.

Ten years ago I converted from Ravidasi Sikh to Christianity. The pastor is also a converted Christian. The reason being our *bhavans* are so sexist that they expect women to make '*langar*' [food] and be silent partners to men. Not a single woman has been on the management committee of a *bhavan* and there is so much petty politics and men play their little power games. Nobody cares for the *sangat* and there is little spirituality.

She continued:

Yes, Jesus Christ is a true God. Proof is that miracles and healing powers are due to his grace. My problems have been solved since I converted to Christianity and by worshiping Jesus Christ. Before that I used to go to *gurdwaras* but did not find peace of mind. They do not want to know your personal problems. They do not even try.

I had a lot of problems with my stomach and doctors did not heal me; but now I am cured of all these ailments. One day they prayed for me in our church and my pain disappeared. A pastor from Ireland asked us to come forward and I did. The lump in my stomach has gone smaller since then. The snake, which used to accompany me everywhere, has also parted company, though it was a good companion. [*I was very surprised to hear this but did not want to question her on this episode.*]

P went on:

You have faith in Jesus and then we are all brothers and sisters in Him. My own family, for instance, my sister goes to church and she has been cured. My son who was in Chandigarh studying a computer course was going to give it up and go home. When we prayed in the church he was happy to stay and continued his studies there.

In my church they really care for me and my family. There are faith healing sessions which I regularly attended. My parents also embraced my religion and they were also cured of their chronic illnesses. My family – back in India – also embraced my religion and has been happy since. Jesus preached love for all mankind and we have so many different nationalities and no body bothers about caste or which part of the world you come from.

In Indian places of worship they want to establish first which caste you belong to. [*How do they do that*?] By asking personal questions such as: What is your surname? Which village do you come from? Which *gurdwara* you or your parents used to go to? This is quite stupid and I hated that. There is no nonsense like this in our church. Every one is treated with respect. When you have personal problems the pastors and others help you enormously and they even financially support the needy. I am totally committed to my religion and go to other people's houses to pray for peace and harmony.

As regards caste relationship, I would say that the next-generation [meaning second and third] do not care much about it. Chamar boys are educated and getting married to Jat girls – the parents cannot do much about it as the young people know their rights in this country.

I greatly admire Mayawati (Chief Minister of UP) who has achieved this high position despite so many hurdles and caste discrimination. She was proclaimed as a heroine when she challenged a high court judge who called her 'Harijan'. She responded who are you to address me in such a condescending language? [*Why?*] As you know Harijan is a label given to us by Gandhi to patronize our community and to keep us within the Hindu fold … I also think highly of Kanshi Ram who was a great politician and laid the groundwork for the victory of Mayawati. [*What about her super affluence?*]. All Indian politicians are rich and they have not become so by fair means. So what if she also follows in their footsteps? I am very proud of her. She might yet become Prime Minister of India if her party wins enough seats in 2008!

I think the caste system will disappear in a few generations in the UK, but In India I am very doubtful. But one thing is there: our community is proud of its success and no longer depends on Jat farmers in villages. Our people have bought land and are saying to Jats: 'come and work on our land.' We are as good as you are.

She wants to open an eating place in a big town but there is no capital to back it up. Her own boy is not too well and has a bullet in his leg and her two estranged daughters have cut off all connections with her because of the abuse in the family. She does look after her elderly parents.

Christian Service in Punjabi, August 2006

P and I went to the church service with her two friends Kusum (K) and Nalini at 5 p.m. The service lasted for two hours and was conducted by a Punjabi-speaking pastor from Pakistan. There was another pastor from Lyallpur now known as Faisalabad. He spoke beautiful Punjabi and gave a well reasoned sermon. Over half the *sangat* was composed of Dalit women who also seemed to have health problems. There were several children as well.

Dalits feel free here as there are 18 nationalities represented in the church so the ideology of caste does not carry any significance. The singing was in Punjabi and so were all the sermons. There were personal prayers and healings. There was tea and samosas after the service. The lady pastor is Irish and married to A … Singh, a Punjabi Christian. P's brother and grandmother were also there. They all seemed to be happy and joyous. One of the pastors has changed his name from Singh to John.

K's dad is also turning to the church. K is also thinking of joining the choir. Pastor Terry told us a story[6] which shocked every one over the dire predicament of Dalit Christians in his country of origin. According to him a couple quarrelled over a minor matter and the wife burnt a copy of the Koran and then made a hue and cry and told the villagers that her husband had done it. The villagers burnt him alive. He continued: 'There are grave injustices in the society where Dalits are treated as serfs and servants. Once with the aid and collaboration of police they burnt the whole village because they blasphemed against the prophet Mohammed. News of such events should be broadcasted to the world.'

Nalini's grandmother is an 82-year-old lady who also attended the Church. She came to this country some 50 years ago and now has great-grandchildren. They have all become Christians, except her parents. Nalini said her grandmother feels confused and now wants to die in peace. I suppose there is little she can tell me about her past. Her memory is fading but she is well looked after by the family.

P's Partner's Views

I have never bothered about caste in my relationships. Since Indian independence we have become a secular nation and want to get rid of such evils as untouchability and religious bigotry. I have friends of all races, religions, and castes in England, India, and elsewhere. Regrettably, the caste card is being played both by high-caste people and Dalits in the UK and India. In this country *gurdwaras* are along caste lines (which reinforce the caste system) as are virtually most arranged marriages. *Biraderi* plays its part in keeping the system going. Regarding my personal relationship, P was sensitive about her caste and I noticed it in our earlier courtship days. I give you an example. She used to play hymns of saint Kabir very frequently and I asked her to play hymns of other saints and gurus. She snapped at me saying: 'you don't want to listen to low-caste hymns.' I was quite shocked to hear this. I explained to her that saint Kabir is revered and respected in the Sikh community and how could she attribute such a charge to me. Then she realized that I genuinely do not care for such matters as caste. Then there are other events which reflected her sensitivity over caste. On certain occasions, I have to attend social functions on my own due to my involvement in various social activities but she thought I was not taking her as it might cause embarrassment … Our

---

6   It was difficult to verify this story so I leave it to the readers to evaluate its contents in the light of their knowledge and experience.

differences and quarrels are due to personality and temperament and nothing to do with caste. She might attribute it to caste to make me feel guilty, but I can say with a hand on my heart that this thought has never entered my brain. It is a long story and I'd rather not go into it.

In India regrettably the situation is far worse. We encountered caste slights and insults on several occasions that upset me very much. Family and social relationships are within caste and *biraderi* and there may be a token gesture to invite people of other castes. In this respect, Punjabi villages are far worse than towns and cities where caste is of less significance.'

P's friend Gurpreet

Gurpreet's experience of social relationship are from a city where all castes mix well. She had employed people from all castes and her food was cooked by a Mazhabi girl, called Ram Piari.

> I never had any sense of discrimination. I ran a clinic at my house which mainly dealt with 'women's' problems. Abortion and other ailments were quite common.
>
> In villages the situation has not changed. People still discriminate and treat them in a negative way. At marriages and other social occasions they are invited as underlings and given food separately. Also they have separate eating utensils. As regards water, people have their own water pumps. So the old question of using high-caste wells does not arise. But everything is separate in villages.

Her experience of inter-caste marriages was quite illuminating of the situation in the Punjab: 'There are some clandestine inter-caste love marriages but such couples are disowned by their respective community and parents.' She gave us two examples, one of which is of her close relative.

> The boy was from a Jat Singh family and the girl was a Harijan. He had an arranged marriage but he kept in touch with his girlfriend. The girl was so much in love that she vowed to commit suicide. The lad said let us do it together. So they took poison and then they went to the boy's home together. His parents saved the boy but let the girl die – who fell at the gate of boy's house. The police took her to the local hospital where she died.

Gurpreet gave a similar example of an inter-caste couple who went on to commit suicide by throwing themselves on a railway track. Again the boy was saved and the girl perished.

She continued:

> *Gurdwaras* are along caste lines in the Punjab as well, although this is not the principle of the Sikh religion. Kabir *bhagat* came from the weaver caste and

likewise Guru Ravidas is the guru of Chamars. Then there are Mazhabi Singhs, who are traditionally called Churas and so on. They are not treated with respect in Jat *gurdwaras* and that is a problem.

Case Study 6: Retired Scientist

Dr B lives in a modern house on the outskirts of a large city. He retired four years ago after over 35 years of service in further and higher education in the UK, and now devotes his time to a charity which he has established to help disadvantaged young people in India. His three children are now adults and in professional occupations. I have used his own words to describe his caste-related experiences. My comments and observations appear in italics.

> My schooling experience was not too bad but there were many Jat (farmer) people who scoffed at me and said that I would not get very far. Now when I go back they respect me and feel ashamed of their past behaviour. I got admission to the local College in 1959 (in the Punjab) and my tuition and hostel fees were paid by the government scholarship. However, I had to find another 50 Rupees (£3 in 1959) as an admission fee which was paid by a retired army man from my village ... Many other villagers encouraged me to study. I had a full beard and turban in India and was a Sikh [*He showed me his picture*]. That way I could get some respect from my fellow students.

He continued:

> I emigrated to England in 1970 with a BSC degree from the Punjab University which was not recognized in England. Therefore, I could find employment only as a lab technician. I had to pass an exam of the Chartered Scientists to gain admission to study for a MSC degree, which I completed in 1975. Then I enrolled for a PhD in nuclear physics, and completed it in 1983 and obtained a post of research associate at a university. I had full scholarship for my studies and I am very thankful for that. Subsequently, I became head of science at a technical college and remained in the post for 22 years. I took early retirement four years ago at 60 and am now running an educational trust for poor students in India.'
> My marriage was arranged and I have two sons and a daughter – all degree holders. My eldest son met an English girl when he was studying in a university and now they are married. She is a senior immigration officer and they live near ..., and she knows about the caste system and wants to go to India and study it there. Her parents accept us and we have visited their family home. I am very pleased with their success as they earn in excess of £95,000. My other son is a police officer and doing well. My daughter is also a graduate ... My kids do not

care about caste matters as they have not faced any problems or discrimination in the UK.

I joined the management committee of Guru Ravidas Bhavan in 1992 and stayed in this position for 12 years and sorted out their finances and litigation problems; and then I resigned. I established the *bhavan's* practices along the same lines as Sikh *gurdwaras* are run. I did not allow '*sants* and *sadhus*' (holy men) from India to interfere and collect money for dubious causes. *Sadhus* from the Punjab took bucketfuls of money in the name of charity and never were accountable to anybody. The name of the temple is *bhavan* and not *gurdwara* to avoid interference from the SGPC [*Established Sikh committee in Amritsar which is in charge of Sikh gurdwaras*]. Ours is a nationwide movement with some *bhavans* even in France, Germany, Canada, and the USA. There are 19 *bhavans* in the UK and several foreign affiliates and I have written a constitution for them.

The former management committee of the *bhavan* owed seven lakhs Rupees (about £8,000) and had several law suits to deal with. Fresh democratic elections took place in 1998 and then the new constitution was adopted. I dealt with all the outstanding issues successfully.

A big mistake was made by the Jat community in the 1960s that lead to formation of *bhavans* i.e. separate holy places for Chamars and Valmikis. The story is that Jat Sikhs in S ... *gurdwara* would not allow a Punjabi Chamar to serve *Parsad* [holy sweet] or make him a member of the management committee though he was a *pucka* Sikh. It is their fault ... So now Chamars go to their *bhavan/gurdwara* with dignity and pride.

Guru Granth Sahib is a holy book which includes 41 slokas [hymns] of Guru Ravidas ji and we treat it with great respect. Our services are no different from other Sikh *gurdwaras* and this is the long and short of it.

Dr Ambedkar is being treated as a guru (Bhim Ki Jai – victory to Ambedkar) by some members of our community. We (meaning the followers of Guru Ravidas Ji) do not agree with that. He was not a religious leader but a political leader and a social reformer. A large number of Chamars and others have become *Bodis* [Buddhists] to follow in his footsteps. In my view, they do not know much about Buddhism but are politically motivated. Caste consciousness would disappear in this country in a few generations but in India it would take a very long time ... A law in the UK parliament should help to reduce its impact on the lives of Indians in this country.

Inter-caste and inter-racial marriages are increasing; my eldest son is married to an English girl as I told you. There are quite a few cases of Chamar boys marrying Jat girls and *vice versa* and parents do not always accept such unions and this could be a source of tension between the two communities.

I am now honoured in my village by the people who treated me badly. I also know that there were good people of Jat caste who supported me and encouraged me. A majority, however, obstructed my aspirations and were cynical about my chances of gaining a good job.

Sometimes I wonder about the wisdom of bodies like 'CasteWatch' – with education and economic advancement of our community, caste should wither away but it will take time as it is ingrained ...

A lot of Jat people in this country worked hard and never mixed with anyone outside their caste and retained the 'old' mentality and started insulting us by calling us Chamars and so on ... they could have embraced us and not shunned us. Even now, I feel uncomfortable when I am invited by them on social functions as it is inbred in them to think that we are inferior human beings. So I try to avoid attending such functions. [*This he said with regret and sadness and I was dismayed to hear this from a man of integrity who has done his best to bring the two communities together.*]

Shree Guru Valmiki Sabha and Ravidas Sabha are UK-based associations and coordinate the works of temples and *bhavans*. I have played my part in it. Now I have started a trust to help poor and disadvantaged high school students in India to study in higher educational institutions. This is established in the name of Guru Ravidas Ji.

I did think of working in India, but Jagjiven Ram [famous Dalit Union Minister] told me: 'Are you mad to come back to India? You wear suits, drive cars, and enjoy high self-esteem ... there are plenty of people like you in India.' That 'meeting' put a stop to my aspiration to go and seek employment in India.

Appendix B
Questionnaires for Interviews

Interview questionnaire for Dalits (India)

		Date	
Name		Age	Occupation
Number and age of children		Own house/ property	
Schools		Religion	
Guru Ravidas		Baba Sahib Dr Ambedkar	
Attitudes of and to Jats and Brahmins		Ad Dharam/Mangoo Ram	
Problems: finance, books etc.		Treatment of boys and girls	
Aspirations		Other caste children	
Teachers' attitude		Do you visit school?	
Caste equality		Inter-marriages	
Experience of caste prejudice		Parents' experience of caste	
Women's position			
Political views		Future of caste systems	
Leadership issues		Dalits abroad	
Relatives/how far?		Their jobs	
Organization			

Interview Questionnaire for Other Castes   **Date**

Name:	Age:	Caste/religion:
Job:	Married children:	House/farm:
Schools:	Aspirations:	
Inter-caste relations:	Ad Dharm/Mangoo Ram:	
Attitudes of Dalits:	Attitudes of higher castes:	OBC:
Dr Ambedkar:	Pollution/purity:	Inter-marriages:
Dalits abroad:	Politics of caste:	Village/local/central:
Future of caste system:		Past injustices:

Teachers' Interview Schedule   **Date:**

1   Teaching Experience

2   Performance of Asian students

3   Aspiration of Asian students – any class/caste differences?

4   Parental attitudes towards education of girls

5   Girls' participation in school life

6   Are you aware of the caste system?

7   If so, does it cause any behavioural problems in schools?

8   Have you had any complaints from girls or their parents based on caste bullying?

9   Do you think there should be school policy on 'caste' similar to race?

10   Should caste awareness/ knowledge be taught in school?

11   If so, which subject should cover it?

12   Any other comments on Asian/Indian girls

Interview	**Questionnaire for Students**	Date

1   Age

2   Parents' jobs

3   Do you have a computer at home?

4   Do you get any help with your home work?

5   Your favourite subjects

6   What do you want to do when you leave school?

7   Occupational aspirations

8   Equality with boys at home

9   Attendance at temple

10   Language spoken at home

11   Have you been back to India? If so, tell me about your stay.

12   Have you heard/read of Indian caste system? If so, elaborate.

13   Do your parents talk about it?

14   Have you ever had any problems, which relate to your caste – such as bullying, teasing ... .

15   Do you consider yourself as Indian/British/ British Asian or Sikh/Hindu ... In terms of your identity?

16   Other comments

Author Index

Subject Index

—